Handle Your Business

Power Moves to Make Your Business Dreams Come True

Toni Moore

HANDLE YOUR BUSINESS
Copyright © 2018 Toni Moore Enterprises

ISBN: 978-1-5136-3233-9

DEDICATION

This book is dedicated to all the men, women and children who are fully committed to making their business dreams a reality.

Legal Notice

PREFACE

"I spent my entire life working for the Company and they fired me! I sucked up to the most stuck up people, smiled away my tears when I got passed over for the senior positions, trained people who ended up being my supervisors, and stayed long nights week after week so much that my days transformed into weeks, months and years."

As my girlfriend paced angrily in my office, I knew she had reached the point of no return. But I didn't know what to say or do to help her appreciate that she finally had what she wanted, the time to create her business. She had worked so hard to salvage her grades in high school and college. She had spent long nights to learn the complexities of finance—the very things that rich men had whispered over on golf courses, in bars and in the coveted Country Clubs.

She didn't need me to be the Bible thumping sage who reminded her that, "God works in mysterious ways." Nor did I want to become the legal strategist that offered advice by referencing federal statutes that were created to protect men/women over 40 years old from workplace discrimination, such as Title VII that protected individuals from racial, sexual and ethnic discrimination or the Age Discrimination Act.

I knew just being a woman wouldn't be sufficient to establish wrongful discharge. But legal precedence had shown me that dismissal of the only woman of color working in a very powerful position at a Fortune 500 did not prove wrongdoing. While everyone knew of the backstabbing and the back working wherein the junior associates and their sponsors would do anything to make her seem less fit. Even the repeated pointing out of every typographical error as though it was monumental despite the continued material mistakes would make a reasonable person question motive.

Based on everything I knew about my friend's issues with her job, I knew there were a few legal arguments we could use if she wanted to pursue an unlawful discharge claim. But I really wanted her to consider taking the severance package which included letters of recommendation from upper management that she could leverage if she decided to start her own business

What I've learned through the years of counseling and advising ambitious individuals is that there is nothing new under the sun, except what we choose to do when the Divine opens the windows of opportunity. More specifically, life doesn't happen to you, but manifested through you based on your decisions within each moment of every day.

Accordingly, if you want something bad enough, you shouldn't wait to receive it nor should you wait for permission to step towards it. Instead, you must appreciate that your desires lead to your destiny.

As I consoled my childhood friend for the loss of her dreams to move up the corporate ranks and eventually become partner, I also reminded her that she didn't really care for the job. I reminded her of the past two years when she repeatedly wondered aloud why she was still at the job. I reminded her of her constant struggle with the back stabbing department who always tried to take bigger cases from her and repeatedly negated her brilliance to potential clients whenever they could. I also reminded her that as a mid-level executive, she was entitled to a sizable severance that would allow her to finally figure out what she wanted out of life.

But more importantly, I encouraged her to appreciate the opportunity to finally create and build the business of her dreams. She no longer had to hide her brilliance so as not to seem as a threat to the members of the Boys Club. Nor did my friend have to tip toe in stilettos so as not to step on anyone's toes. Nor did the corporate class ceiling have the power to limit her from manifesting a greater destiny.

I watched her and listened to fear take hold of my friend. I had seen it before as fear once controlled me. And I've watched as fear kept many brilliant men and women in "their places" at jobs that paid them pittance in comparison for their true worth. Before she could go into another bout of woe is me, I appealed to her inner boss and made a case as to why she should step into greater and seize the moment. The Universe finally heard her cries and I felt divinely inspired to make a case for her to unleash her greatness from a high paying version of an indentured servant.

7

I told her to find the courage she needed to live her dreams, discover the tribe that finally got her vibe and to appreciate her inner power to create the life she loved. I knew if she only saw the break in employment as a curse, she would never appreciate the blessing of finally getting a break to breathe.

For more than 10 years, she climbed the corporate ladder, took on more assignments than the law should allow and sacrificed play time to show up to appease those who used and abused her. So I reminded her that the same gifts, talents and abilities she used in her job would be assets in her own business. And I reminded her that her job never asked her to sign a Noncompete Agreement so there was no reason why she couldn't contact her clients and spin the departure as though it were her idea.

As I imagined what she could do with her life once she appreciated that she was more than enough to overcome any obstacles, I smiled at her. In response, she looked at me as though I was the one who needed pity. In a last ditch effort, I reminded her of the fact that she had access to state unemployment benefits that seeded into employees turned entrepreneurs, wisdom within her reach from retirees at SCORE, potential clients she served through the years, her sponsor who always offered her assistance and me, her bestie legal strategist who was more than willing to introduce her to the local business community.

After listening to my heartfelt pleas of giving her business dreams a chance despite her circumstance, I saw a sparkle of hope in my friend's teary eyes. The conversation that first began as a legal consultation to a possible wrongful discharge lawsuit transformed into a legal strategy session about making her business dreams a reality.

Table of Contents

INTRODUCTION

So you say you want to start a business? Well, good for you. Now before you start hiring coaches, getting branded or hiring a virtual assistant, you must get crystal clear about who you are, who you help, how you help and what others will say yes to. You may also teach yourself how to learn the numbers with regards to cash flow statements, balance sheets and income statements. You may also want to learn about the rules and regulations that's regulating your particular line of business and your copyright. Think more about the name of your organization, your business friendship, potential partners and who is going to be on your team as you make your business dreams a reality.

In the past twenty plus years of legal experience serving as advocate, counselor, strategist and shoulder to cry on, I've learned there are so many women who decide that they want to start a business, make money and build empires from their desires, but forget the little things.

I have started several businesses and even went into the multi-level marketing Arena; Primerica, Tracy Lynn, 5 Links and Paparazzi. But when it came to sharing my brilliance in my brilliantly branded business, I limited myself. And that's why I wrote this book because without clarity of what you need you'll continually fail. And I'm not talking clarity about color, brand logo, graphic meme or marketing strategy. I'm talking about gaining clarity as the Savvy CEO of your life, business and legacy who is more than enough to make your business dreams possible.

In creating, building, growing and protecting your business, you need clarity with regards to the profit margin statements. You need clarity with regards to the finance market. You need clarity regarding your audience. And you need clarity regarding the legalities governing your realities in your small business. What I know for sure, we don't have to lose everything the first time to get it right the second time.

Many people have dreams of having their own business for many reasons. Some people want to make money and make something of themselves. Others want to be able to supplement their income. And still others want the freedom to monetize their brilliance without limitation. Whatever the reason you want to start a business, always begin doing it the right way, and keep running it with good intentions.

One popular belief is that you need tons of experience, expertise, and knowledge to start a business. The opposite is true. While it helps to go to school and learn the tricks of the trade, it does not necessarily mean that you cannot start a business if you do not have a degree. In fact, the opposite is seemingly true because not having a comfortable JOB gives tons of individuals the boost they need to figure out the own formula for success.

And while law can be overwhelming to most lay people, you can't ignore the "legal mumbo jumbo" when starting and building your business. More specifically, in building your business, you must consider corporate law, contracts, business ethics, criminal code, IP, franchising and accidental franchising arrangements, antitrust issues, employment, tax issues and possible tort claims that include slander, defamation and libel. I'm sure my legal brethren and sisters would add even more.

Even if you're coaching, speaking and serving in a transformational capacity, you must still acknowledge and appreciate IRS, EEOC, FTC, DOL and SEC rules and regulations; more information in the reference section. I won't even get into literary rights or copyright issues most people fail to appreciate when creating blogs, writing memoirs or using other people's music in videos, presentations, conferences and live streams since that would entail a whole lecture on the Copyright Act of 1976 from the literary and musical perspective.

Believe me, if you're working with others, making monetization promises, hiring others (whether paid or unpaid), or selling any products or services, you must appreciate the legalities governing your realities. Sorry, but not sorry.

Instead, when you're in business you must handle business as a responsible business executive even if you do not know the rules and regulations. More specifically, did you know that once you start a sole proprietorship or single person LLC, you are responsible for taking care of business, covering your assets and knowing the rules and regulations governing your business?

Similarly, if you start a corporation (whether for or nonprofit), you are responsible for governance of every aspect of the business; including complying with the law. And yes that includes overseeing the mission, vision, programs, budgets and everything else in between.

I'm sure most people have a friend who can help them start a business. If you don't have a sister, cousin or business associate, you can go online and get someone to fill out a few corporate forms and voila you're in business. Just know, if running a business was about filling out forms, big business wouldn't have a board, compliance officers, corporate counsel, in-house legal departments AND outside legal counsel.

So my question to you is if you are in the business game to play business everyone else thinks you should? Don't answer right now because your ego will convince you that you're right. The important things to remember are that you need to research, ask the right questions, and get the best advice you can.

The purpose of this book is to address your basic legal issues in creating and building your dream business. The first part of the book addresses mindset issues that you will encounter when you transform your employee mindset to a CEO mindset. The second part of the book entails fundamental decisions you need to make for your business--from choosing the problem you want to solve, to the type of client you want to attract. And the third part of the book covers the legalities that govern your business realities.

In the pages that follow, you will find straight-forward information that has helped thousands of entrepreneurs make their business dreams a reality. In fact, as I wrote the book, I pulled some information from my talks with small business owners, some social media posts and in a few instances some responses to direct messages. Throughout this book, you will be given information to play a smarter business game to ensure you uplevel your success... legally of course.

HUMBLE BEGINNINGS

I once worked at a law firm wherein anytime I asked my supervisor for assistance, he would ask me what I would do if I was the boss. No matter the issue; whether I was having problems with irate clients, argumentative lawyers, non-payment of fees or career decisions, he would always redirect my questions back to me. After a few months of questioning and redirection, I stopped asking him for guidance and started doing as though I was the boss. No one else knew the quandary I was having since I was usually the main point of contact. However, I needed to convince myself that I was more than capable of making the right decisions.

Similar to many women who lived before me, I was never really given an opportunity to step into my power. Instead, I had gone through so much as a child that I didn't know what my real voice sounded like and had lost track of my vision. Accordingly, I stopped myself from speaking, and waited for permission on the things that mattered most to me.

The same thing happened in my profession. I roared like a lion in the courtroom, but raised my hand to ask a question in the boardroom. Every once in a while, I would forget that I was a lady who was expected to sacrifice for others and I would boss up despite the consequence for overstepping an imaginary line. So as not to be deemed a troublemaker, I would apologize and do whatever I could to prove that I truly was a team player who was ready, willing and able to sacrifice for the team.

That all changed, however, when my boss no longer wanted to oversee the general practice that serviced the prepaid legal plans. Once I started stepping into the role as decision maker at the firm, I started evaluating my role as a wife, mother, daughter, sister, volunteer, church member and friend. Slowly, but surely, I began making decisions so that I could achieve better results in every aspect of my life. I began firing some people, promoting some people, transferring some people and even demoting some people. And when new people showed up, I assessed them to find out their goals, intentions and aspirations.

I later left the firm which was a huge surprise to most, but not to those who appreciated that I had decided to reclaim my power to ensure my voice, vision and vocation mattered to me. I figured if companies could reorganize by filing for Bankruptcy, I could reorganize my life by letting go of what no longer worked for me.

I later learned that creating and running a business was a whole lot different than working as an employee. So I did like so many others do and began asking friends and family how to build a profitable business. Some people told me to go to conferences, so I went to conferences. Others told me to hire a business coach, so I hired a few coaches. And still others told me that I needed to create a brand, build a website, establish a mailing list and get on social media to do live streaming every day.

I never really connected the dots until I took a moment for myself to assess where I was, where I wanted to be and what, if anything, I had accomplished. Of course I wanted to make money, but making money wasn't the primary reason to leave a good paying job to leap into the edge of my reality.

Similar to many womenpreneurs, I wanted the autonomy to become the fullest expression of myself. I wanted to help people I felt I was called to serve. I wanted the freedom to choose how I was going to show up in the marketplace. I didn't want to be boxed into a profession or limited to how I could serve others because of my degree.

I knew deep down on the inside that those who looked like me talk like me and started with nothing but a dream similar to me were not cultivated to be creators, but employees. I wanted to be the guide who helped others get to the other side of their breakdowns. In taking an assessment of my life, I notice how others were going through the same trials, tribulations and setbacks as I had. And I wanted to help.

I saw first-hand what happens when people who are selected to lead aren't in the right position thus causing others to fail. And I also saw how others stopped themselves from having, doing and being because of not knowing what to do next. So after I almost lost my life by trying to cover-up an ectopic pregnancy (another book), I took a leap of faith to create a business and life that reflected my dreams.

Unfortunately, things got tricky because I knew I wanted to inspire and empower women, but my habits, rituals and patterns were based on how I saw other people do. Similar to many womenpreneurs, I tried to define my start based on another person's well-tailored, cultivated and tweaked portrayals of their "success." But after stopping and starting, stopping and starting again, I finally realized that I was responsible for doing whatever it took to make my business dreams a reality. Similarly, you must do whatever it takes to ensure you show up as your best empowered self.

BOSS UP YOUR MIND

If you want to be happy and live the life of your dreams, you must appreciate that the life you live is based on your actions, inactions, reactions and responses. Throughout my talks and coaching sessions, people often tell me why they haven't or why they can't get over the pain of sexual abuse, mental abuse, discrimination and racism. Some even e-mail me about the trauma of not having, not knowing and not becoming because of what happened in their past. After hugging some and touching and agreeing with others, I look them squarely in their eyes and ask them whether or not they are okay with being a whiner throughout their life or if they truly want to win

While I empathize with them, I know I only have a few moments to awaken them from their spiritual slumber. Accordingly, I do whatever it takes to jolt them awake in hopes that their response will inspire them to assess whether or not the life they live is the life they love. Even in my own victim to victorious transformation, I had to transform shelf help into self-help. In fact, the first shelf help book I ever read was, *Woman Thou Art Loosed* by Bishop T.D. Jakes. After reading that book, I found myself wondering what I needed to be loosed from. And more importantly, whether or not I was keeping myself from living my best life by holding on to something that wasn't meant for me.

What I've learned in my journey to becoming my best self is that we weren't cultivated to be the bosses of our creativity. Instead, we were cultivated to work hard, and appease those who are in charge of our education, careers and spiritual livelihood, and socio-economic status.

Because we have been cultivated to do as others say, we often fail to take much needed radical action to transform our reality. Even statistics substantiates the stories we tell ourselves of what we can't do based on what others won't do. In fact, according to the Centers for Disease Control and Prevention, neglect, physical abuse, custodial interference, and sexual abuse are types of child maltreatment that can lead to poor physical and mental health well into adulthood. Very few parents cultivate their children to be bold and brilliant enough to make life beautiful based on their DNA (desires, needs and abilities).

Instead, generation after generation are taught how to deal with the lies of life by sitting down, getting educated, getting a job, career or spouse and being content with what life offered. In effect, our man pleasing, id protecting ego dictates our footsteps thus negating the essence of who we truly are. By cultivating our ego more than our essence, we also unconsciously control, alter and delete our infinite possibilities of fulfilling a greater destiny.

As children we got away with blaming others for not giving us what we needed to discover our strengths, weaknesses, abilities and gifts. But when you are in business, you must boss up your mind. You must continually decree, declare and do the extraordinary to change what is perceived as ordinary. You must talk about yourself. You must shine the light on you. You must brag a little about how you've helped others. And you must be willing to say no to the people, places and things who refuse to say yes to you.

When you don't appreciate that you are more than enough to be good enough, pretty enough or worthy enough to get what you want, you will fail to make your business dreams a reality. Similarly, when you don't speak what you seek, you sabotage the possibilities of what could be because you dim the light within you. Or worse yet, you show up as a spectator instead of as a participant who is fully empowered to actualize what you visualize by manifesting what you speak. Unfortunately, when

23

you fail to show up as the person you were born to be, you fail to become the person you need to be to achieve what was meant to be.

Never forget, at the end of your day God, the Source, Divine, the BOSS of all things will judge what you accomplished based on what He put in you, spoke over you and expected from you. Accordingly, to make your business dreams a reality, you must become the boss of your mind. You should also stop blaming yourself when others don't appreciate who you are because some will, some won't and some just will never care. You should also stop punishing yourself for what you did in the past because you can't have a prosperous future if you have a prodigal mindset.

What I know for sure, everything is foundational. So as you overcome the little things in life, you will discover that there is nothing new under the sun. More specifically, the same way you had to learn, unlearn and overcome in your former years is the same way you must do in your latter years. Thankfully, the quicker you learn from your mistakes, the quicker you get through the obstacles to get to what's meant for you; peace, joy and happiness in every aspect of your life.

BIRTH YOUR BRILLIANCE

As children we often heard that we should sit down, shut up, be still and act nice. In response, we earned the grades, achieved the awards and attained the high honors in hopes of being noticed by our parents or caretakers. Similarly during our adolescent years, we learned to make the right moves to be appreciated and adored by those who mattered to us. Even throughout adulthood, we found ourselves seeking ways to attract the attention of the masses so that our voices mattered.

Unfortunately, no one really asked us what we desired, what we needed to love our lives, about our aspirations or cultivate our limitless possibilities. Nor did anyone prepare us to unleash our success by sharing the secret to success; staying true to our dreams.

Instead, those who were smarter, prettier, skinnier and talented were pushed toward those in power in hopes that they would be chosen to bring success to the family. All others who didn't come from the right families or didn't have the right sponsors to support them were either ignored or given just enough support so as not to be deemed as abuse. Or worse yet, castigated to the peripheries of society as unworthy, uncontrollable or incorrigible.

In effect, many of us grew up thinking that we must appease others by looking like them, talking like them, walking like them, dressing like them and agreeing with them in order to live like them. In doing so, we did more for others to hear the sound of their approval than we did to appease the murmurings of our heart.

And while nothing is wrong with wanting to be loved and appreciated by others, it should never come to a point that we allow someone else's response to matter more than the words God etched into our hearts.

During my formative years, I watched my mother play the victim role wherein she never had the singing career she wanted, never had the marriage she wanted or the love she wanted. While I vowed never to be a woman like my mother, I found myself going through some of the things she went through. I had endured a lot of physical, mental and sexual abuse from others so much so that I started to abuse myself by objectifying myself.

Throughout the in between I started way too many businesses based on what another promised in hopes that somehow their magic would rub off on me. But none did. I later questioned my footsteps and parked myself in neutral in hopes that someone would activate something for me to help me live a better life. But none did.

Through many tests, trials and tribulations, I stumbled upon my inner spark of God that empowered me to manifest my dreams. After testing the waters, failing a few times and pushing myself past my realities, I discovered that we have the power to change our life beyond our wildest dreams. Similarly, your potential to achieve greatness isn't limited by the negativity you encounter or the abuse you endure. Even in its dormant state, your brilliance shines deep down on the inside waiting for you to seek it, embrace it and harness its energy to transform our good works into greater works.

As with anything in life, the first step to building your dream business is to believe in you. You must be still and know that you were fearfully and wonderfully made to live your dreams. You must also give yourself permission to take a leap of faith to go beyond your comfort zone.

As you begin putting one foot in front of the other, your newfound thoughts about who you are motivates your movements to seek, know and ask for more. As you know more, you find yourself push pass man boundaries in hopes of making what your heart sees your reality. Before you know it, you'll find the strength to fire those who once abused you and find the courage to surround yourself with those who cultivate, celebrate and pay for your willingness to share your brilliance.

Within each new experience, you'll develop more skills and attain more knowledge that empowers you to dominate each subsequent level. You'll also make progress in building the life you love; you rise above the statistics of the status quo that pervades your existence. Similarly, you'll find out more about who you are, who's you are and what else can be.

As you find out more about you the brilliance within you, your likes, dislikes and strength, you'll tap into the endless possibilities within you to monetize your brilliance. By tapping into the brilliance within you, you will continually empower yourself to see what your heart has always seen which motivates you to dream possible and continually go for bigger, better and more than before.

BE A PROBLEM SOLVER

Being in business is about finding solutions. That is what sets the strong businesses apart from the others. You do not want to sell just anything because others are doing it. Instead, you must fully appreciate that your brilliance is custom made to fit someone else's needs.

So before you try to use your brilliance in business, you should take a SWOT analysis of your knowledge, skills and abilities. More specifically determines what your soul CRAVES. What do you wish someone would create, what social and/or public policy issue resonates with you, what do you give your attention to, what do you visualize when you close your eyes to day dream and lastly what did you expect to see as a child?

If a response doesn't exude from your spirit, then I want you to put your mad hat on and identify the problem(s) that vexes you. Are you vexed when kids aren't fed properly? Are you vexed when senior citizens are abused? Are you vexed when a beautician damages another person's hair? Are you vexed when business owners are played by liars and deceivers in the marketplace?

Once you determine the specific problem, issue or cause you want to alleviate, you can look for solutions. You will not find any market without faults. There are plenty of problems that need to be resolved. Even the competition cannot resolve every issue out there. Even if there is someone doing what you want to do, find a way to differentiate yourself and start sharing your brilliance.

When you are passionate about a problem, situation, issue and/or cause, you will be emotionally connected to it. And once you are emotionally connected to it, you will be motivated to continually seek out new ways to open new doors and new opportunities to share your passion. Your passion about something will motivate others to do different. And as you inspire others, you become a respected thought leader who serves as the most-sought after point of contact on a particular issue.

This issue can stem from something they bought somewhere else, or it can be an issue they have had for a period of time and need a solution for it. There may not even be a problem because what others perceived as problematic became a way of life until you showed up.

As you step into the role as problem solver, continually do who what, why and how assessment. Do your own research and development to assess whether a solution to the problem is profitable. Seek to see whether there is a thought leader, author, speaker, or business coach; someone who is an ambassador of the issue. Connect with them, study them and model your business similar to theirs until you can manifest your own recipe for success.

Choose Your Industry Wisely

In choosing your industry, choose an area and/or niche that does not just interest your target market. You should have an interest in it too. More than just a little interest, you need to like the products or services that are out there in the market.

If you do not like the products or services the market has to offer, how will you feel when you are doing business with the people who are interested in them? People will pick up on your superficial interest which can break the business relationships you worked so hard to make. So please do yourself a favor and do not get wrapped up in an industry that you do not have an utmost passion about.

Instead, find your Sweet Spot. When people hear me talk or even ask about someone's sweet spot, they usually think I'm being flirtatious. However, when I redirect them to the place of interest flowing with milk and honey wherein one finds pleasure, peace, joy and happiness, a whole different conversation takes place.

Through the years of seeking, knowing, asking and stumbling through the dark without guidance of a mentor or sponsor, I stumbled upon my Sweet Spot. I've learned that the Sweet Spot is the place where we naturally create intellectual property; ideas and spiritual wisdom, guidance and insight. Once you discover your Sweet Spot, you're less likely to have mind blocks that keep you from appreciating your endless possibilities.

So if you found your Sweet Spot, continuously seek ways to satisfy your craving for more. But if you haven't, take an assessment of your strengths, gifts, talents, services rendered and services offered to ensure you are finding enjoyment while giving, loving and doing unto others to ensure you find enjoyment in doing you.

Build Your Credibility

You need to let people know who you are. This pertains to building relationships with your customers, and since you are new with the business, you will build relationships with potential customers. Spend some time before launching your big business idea learning more about your industry and the people who spend money there.

You can always try selling other people's products first – as an affiliate marketer. I learned about securities, trading and insurance as an affiliate marketer. I also learned about sales formation and connecting with others when I represented another company. When you have enough knowledge and you are talking about the product online (such as on your blog), this will help build street credibility as the people who read it will feel you know what you are talking about.

GET CRYSTAL CLEAR ABOUT YOUR CLIENT

I've heard a marketing quote I've found to be true that says, "If you sell to everyone, you sell to no one." If you've live long enough to want to start a business, leave your job or be the problem solver to a specific problem to help others live better, similar to me, you have found that everyone has their own set of trials, tribulations, wish list of resources and formulas for success. Accordingly, you must get crystal clear on whose problem you want to solve.

Do you want to help aspiring authors who were once battered women? Do you want to help young attorneys think beyond their degrees? Do you want to help women boss up their business through sales?

Each group of individuals have their own trials, tribulations and issues they face on a daily basis. Accordingly, you can't just say that you want to help women of a certain age that makes a certain amount of money. Instead, you must become crystal clear about who, what, when, and why you want to help a particular group of individuals.

Without being this specific, you will be a, "buy my stuff," type of entrepreneur who just talks because others are talking. And you will attract general spectators who will fill up your discovery session because it's free, or because they like your personality. In effect, you fill your schedule offering discovery sessions to less-than-ideal clients, will sell fewer memberships, waste time on marketing and discovery, and spend way too much money serving trying to speak on Virtual Stages in hopes that somehow, someway people will see you, know you, like you and purchase from you. Trust me when I say, been there, done that and have several t-shirts from past conferences, masterminds and boot camps.

All that wasted time and money leads to frustration and a sense of despair, not only for you, but for those you're communicating with as well. Think about it. If you continually receive marketing messages from someone who is clearly not resonating with you, how does that make you feel? Don't do that to your potential clients.

Instead, concentrate on narrowing your focus to that one ideal client who desperately needs your help, and with whom you have a clear connection. When you get this part right, you'll build a list of active, responsive prospects who eagerly seek out your newest products and programs, and who will happily buy everything in your funnel.

Now, how do you discover your ideal client? That's easy; stalk them to learn more about them. Seriously, find out more about their interests. Do some research to figure who they like, who they follow, what resonates with them. If you already know them or know their interests, then you are ahead of the game. Of course, since you are the expert in your niche, or trying to be, you will know a lot about their interests already.

You can do some research on social media to find out what their interests are as well. Facebook has groups and so does Twitter. Find a group related to your niche and observe it to see what people are talking about. Use this as advice on what types of products or services to market as well.

The best advice for using social media groups to learn more about your target audience is not to join any group and post on their asking all kinds of questions. For instance, you don't want to join a group and then ask everyone to give their opinion about their favorite game, or gadget. Just observe first, and then engage in the conversation as you would with a friend. Get to know people first, and then ask them questions here and there.

To help you get started, think about your current clients. Who among them is your favorite? What is it about her that makes you happy to get on the phone with her? Who do you dislike? Maybe she fails to follow through with assignments, or pushes back on every suggestion you make, or maybe you simply aren't excited about her business model.

Next, think about what angers you in your niche. When you're passionate about a particular group of people, you'll often find yourself standing up for them when you see them being mistreated. For example, one long-time business coach has a heart for stay-at-home moms. She wants to see them succeed in business, and she's angered (maybe even enraged) by multi-level-marketing companies that take advantage of this market. And she is showing up every day helping her target market helping them to see their endless possibilities.

Another savvy CEO has discovered that her name means everything. Accordingly, she is teaching her target audience to appreciate their name, their value and their vision. And another savvy CEO is helping entrepreneurs obtain celebrity attachment so that they can show up brilliantly in the coaching community. Now it's your turn, get crystal clear about your client and help them make their dreams come true.

BE THE VOICE

What societal issue, problem or deficit you wish could be changed? Take a moment to really think about it, think of the things in your community or even in your society that seemingly serves as a stumbling block. When identifying the problem, consider two things: we are creatures of habit and thus are not willing to change-- unless we are motivated to do so.

Accordingly, when identifying the problem, ensure that it is something that fills one of the following needs: emotional, educational, economic or spiritual need. If you can't identify the issue in a way that resonates with you, it won't resonate with the people you feel you can properly serve.

And if you are just operating from a merely logical perspective, it will be hard to effectuate the type of change that will arise to the level it needs to be to become a public issue wherein policy makers will stand behind it. However, if you get enough people to buy into your vision and mission, you could very well be the catalyst that ultimately changes the trajectory of another's destiny for good.

To help you become the voice of change follow these steps:

1. Define the problem: In defining the problem, write it as a wish list wherein if money was not an issue you would commit your time and energy to it from the beginning to its end. In identifying this project, define it in a clear and concise manner so that when you share it with others who want to help you as much as they can.

2. Express your vision: Do some research to share why the defined problem serves as a stumbling block. Describe what life could look like if the problem was no longer an issue in society.

3. Tell your story: Why does resolving the problem matter so much to you? How did or does this issue affect you? Does it keep you up at night? What would life look like to you if the societal problem was no longer an issue?

4. Develop evidence to substantiate your claim: Do some research, consider the rules, regulations, other people working on the problem and pinpoint what else is missing

5. Assemble the alternatives: Discuss what may happen if society continues to do what it does without change; raise the issue if extremist gets involved and then build a case to substantiate why your solution is the best solution to turn things around.

6. Present the Cost-Benefit Analysis: People are less likely to support your project unless they are getting some benefit out of helping you. Accordingly, identify the cost of not doing in quantitative numbers, the benefit of helping out with making change possible and discuss the possibility of what else could be once the project has been eradicated.

7. Find Supporters: Teamwork makes the dream work because the more eyes you have on the problem, the more you can attack the issue so that it's no longer a problem. Additionally, each of us was wonderfully and fearfully made with a gift, talent and/or

ability to change our reality. Accordingly, give people the opportunity to help make change possible.

8. Launch the Project: Once you have clearly identified the problem, researched the possibilities of doing nothing, doing differently and making change happen, share it with others. Even if it's to perfect, launch it anyway because experience is your best teacher and nothing happens if you continually think about it.

9. Assess your footsteps, revise and continually share until your good is better and your better, greater.

As you can see, you have everything you need to make your voice, vision and dreams matter. But you must step up and stand out boldly. You must do what you need to do to make your dreams come true. And you must use your voice to speak what you seek to convince others that the best way to make change possible is to manifest what you said.

SHOWCASE YOUR BRILLIANCE

I'm sure you heard it enough times that people only do business with those who they like, know and trust, but I'm going to tell you again. If people don't know, like or trust you, they will not buy from you. Accordingly, you must make it a priority to introduce yourself to your prospective clients so that they see you as the resource to helping them soothe a pain or satisfy a need. In so doing, you must leverage who you know, your access to social media and to continually show up as the spokesperson for your company's products and services.

In some way or the other, all social networking sites allow you to build communities. People are asked to become members and write about their interests and hobbies in their profiles. Now, these automatically become searchable keywords. If you are running a business about crocheting, simply type 'crocheting' in the search bar and you will get a whole list of people who are interested in crocheting. Invite them to your community. Discuss crocheting and make them realize that you know the game. When you recommend a product to them after gaining their trust, it is quite likely that they will go ahead and purchase your stuff. Just pick something and become the ambassador of it.

You must not only be active on social networking sites, you must be purposeful. Accordingly, introduce yourself as the go-to expert that helps your target audience do whatever your big promise is. Then speak about what you do, inform people, give them reviews and they will be hooked. It's also a good idea to be the most relevant expert in the room instead of the smartest person because most people like to consult with people who gets, likes and knows them.

In showing up as the go-to expert, you must make every effort to dominate your zone of genius to ensure you are number 1 in your field of expertise. Trust, if you show up as a No. 2, you will more than likely be passed over whenever the No. 1 expert in your field is available.

To ensure you stand out from the rest of similarly situated experts in your field, I suggest you dominate the marketplace so much so that when your ideal client and/or target audience seek your first, create a web presence. Whether you use a CD, web or print portfolio, it's a great way to showcase the work you've done in the past. In most instances, most people believe that if you've done it for others, you can accomplish the same results for them. In addition, Google likes words and video. Hence, the more you showcase your brilliance online with content, the more likely Google will showcase you.

Create a blog. You need to own yourname.com or a website that aligns with your name in some fashion. Depending on who you are, how much time you have on your hands and if you can accept criticism, you should either start a blog or stick with a static homepage. Those who blog will have a stronger asset than those who don't because blogs rank higher in search engines and lend more to your expertise and interest areas over time.

Create and update your LinkedIn profile. A LinkedIn profile is a combination of a resume, cover letter, references document and a moving and living database of your network. Use it to create your own personal advertising, to search for jobs or meet new people. Additionally, make sure stay connected with your profile to avoid losing business opportunities as I did.

Show up on your Facebook profile. Over 2 billion people have profiles, but almost none of them have branded themselves properly using this medium. Be sure to include a Facebook picture of just you, without any obscene gestures or unnecessary vodka bottles. Also, input your work experience and fill out your profile, while turning on the privacy options that disable the ability for people to tag you in pictures and videos, (allowing people to see the ones tagged of you).

Become a thought-leader on Twitter. Your Twitter profile should have an avatar that is carved out of your Facebook picture and used in your LinkedIn profile. You need to use a distinct background, fill out your profile and include a link to either your blog or LinkedIn profile.

Create a video resume on YouTube. A video resume is a short video of you talking about why you are the best for a specific job opportunity. You get about a minute or so to communicate your brand and are able to send the link, once you upload it to YouTube, to hiring managers.

Select clothing that make you look like a thought-leader in your chosen field. Always remember, your personal style is tangible and is extremely important for standing out from the crowd. Select clothing that best represents you because it will be viewable through your pictures/avatars online, as well as when you meet people in reality.

Create a professional e-mail address. Most people use e-mail over all social networks and when you connect with someone on a social network, you are notified via e-mail, so get used to it. Your e-mail address poses a great opportunity for your brand. I recommend getting youname.com and setting up an e-mail in info@yourname.com. While Google e-mail is acceptable in most places, it speaks volumes to people who don't quite appreciate that in business reducing overhead expenses is key to making your business dreams a reality.

CHOOSE THE RIGHT PARTNER

Business partners often start businesses together with little planning and few ground rules. Sooner or later, they discover the hard way that what's left unsaid or unplanned often leads to unmet expectations, anger and frustration. Partners can clash over countless things, including conflicting work ethics and financial goals, roles in the business and leadership styles. And much like marriages, a break-up in business can be just as bad or worse than a long-drawn out divorce. Accordingly, before you partner with a tall, dark and handsome partner with deep pockets, a childhood friend, business bestie or lover, I want you to consider a few things.

First, ask yourself: Do I really need a business partner to build a successful company? Taking on business partners should be reserved for when a partnership is critical to success — say, when the prospective partner has financial resources, connections or vital skills you lack. You may be better off hiring the other person as an employee or an independent contractor.

Communication is important at every stage of a partnership, and especially so at the outset. A common mistake business partners make is jumping into business before really getting to know each other. You must be able to connect to feel comfortable expressing your opinions, ideas and expectations.

If you haven't worked together previously, test the partnership out by tackling a small project together that showcases each other's skills and requires cooperation. This is also a way to learn about each other's personality and core values. Ideally partners' professional skills should complement one another, but not overlap too much. For example, you may be detail oriented and your partner may be a big-picture thinker. Or you may be an expert in marketing and sales, while your partner prefers to stay in the backdrop pouring over financials.

To gauge how well you might work together, have a chat with each other's colleagues and family members. Key questions to answer include: Do you and your partner share personal and professional values, ideas and goals? Do you trust your partner's motivations and character? In what areas of everyday life and business do you agree? What if a spouse or kid later wants to join the business? How will it be handled if one partner acts unethically? What if one partner wants to move out of the country?

Approach a partnership with close friends or family as you might with strangers. Thoughtfully plan and prepare for every aspect of it in advance so there's no question about how difficult situations will be handled. Those who succeed often have learned to set boundaries to keep the business from dominating every aspect of their lives. For example, they may have agreed to leave the office at 5 p.m. and put all conversation about work on hold until after the kids are in bed.

Once the decision is made to start a business together, you should create a partnership agreement with help from a lawyer and an accountant. Every agreement should address three crucial areas: compensation, exit clauses, and roles and responsibilities. Include who owns what percentage of the business, who is investing what, where the money is coming from, and how and when partners will be paid.

Typically partners set up equal ownership and each contributes 50% of the initial investment. But terms can vary greatly. For instance, one partner might contribute more money if the other partner can bring in expertise or business contacts. As the business grows and changes, adjust compensation accordingly. For example, partners may agree to work initially without compensation, and to get paid after a certain revenue target is reached. In addition, if the business partnership brings on more people or if a particular partner is putting in more or less time, building some flexibility into the contract can let you adjust payments.

The agreement should also cover how you plan to exit the business. Include clauses that spell out cases in which one partner is obliged to buy out the other's interest — for instance, if one wants to quit the business. For instance, it can state that the other partner must buy him or her out for a negotiated percentage of the business's value. If neither partner wants to continue the business, partners can also liquidate and divide all assets.

It's also a good idea to settle on in advance how to assess the total value of the business upon dissolution. The agreement should specify who appraises the business and the methodology to use. Outline your expectations for how you'll operate your business. Clearly delineate the roles and responsibilities of the partners based on their skills and desires. This will eliminate turf wars and clearly show employees to whom they should report.

Establish routines for daily communication. For example, agree to talk twice a day at designated times and to re-evaluate their goals on a regular basis. At least once a quarter, sit down and discuss how you envision the future of the business and what steps to take in getting there. Addressing these issues up front will help you better focus on your business later. How you work out the details of setting up a partnership could be an indicator of how well or poorly your prospective venture will operate. Inevitably, some potential partners will realize through the process they weren't meant to be.

CHOOSE THE RIGHT BUSINESS STRUCTURE

Structuring your business correctly is a crucial first step in ensuring future success. If you choose an appropriate structure, then you'll be in a position to grow your business without having to deal with the distractions of a change in legal structure. The main structures include sole proprietorship, partnership, corporation and trust. Each of these business structures has advantages and disadvantages.

Sole Proprietor

A sole proprietor structure is simple, cost-effective and easy to set up. If you run a one person service business then setting up as a sole trader makes a lot of sense. Two key issues with a sole trader structure are that the business revenue is personal income, and your personal liability is not limited.

This is the most basic structure. You became a sole proprietor the minute you hung out your shingle, whether that was on the Web or on the street. You are generally doing business under your own name, and you are the sole owner of that business. Since your sole proprietorship is not a corporation, you don't wind up paying corporate taxes. Instead, you simply pay taxes on the profits of the business. This simplifies the accounting chores a great deal.

A Sole Proprietor may elect to do business under a fictitious name. This is not as sinister as it sounds; it simply means the person in question is doing business under a registered trademark. For example, John Smith may have named his business, "Any town Business Strategist." That would be considered a fictitious name, and his license would say, "John Smith, DBA (Doing Business As) "Any town Business Strategist." This also enables Mr. Smith to open a separate business account at the banking institution of his choice.

The advantages of a Sole Proprietorship: You have the greatest control over business decisions, since typically you have nobody else to answer to. A Sole Proprietorship is easily formed and dissolved, requiring little in the way of legal formalities. Accounting is much simpler. Tax forms are usually only 1-2 pages long, and recent changes in tax laws allow Sole Proprietors to file annually instead of quarterly. A Sole Proprietorship is subject to very little in the way of government regulations. Company profits go directly to the business owner.

Disadvantages of a Sole Proprietorship: Raising capital is more difficult, since you cannot sell shares of the company, and a Sole Proprietorship has a smaller degree of perceived "legitimacy" than a corporation or an LLC. It is more difficult to secure bank financing. Hiring of employees can be more of a problem. You can be subject to both the Federal Tax Rate and a "self-employment tax," effectively being subject to double taxation. The "biggie:" UNLIMITED LIABILITY. This means that if your business is sued, your own personal assets are at risk.

Partnership

With the addition of a partnership there is the opportunity to pool the capital and management resources to grow the business further or to help run the already successfully expanding scenario. There are two very basic types of partnerships and that would the limited partnership and the general partnership. The general partnership is relatively easy to establish as it only requires the names to be included and an agreement to be drawn up stating the various rights and responsibilities of each party within the business partnership platform.

The advantages of the general partnership would include the simplicity of the organization basics, the additional personal resources either financial or managerial in its capacity, the low start-up cost, limited outside regulations and no possibility of double taxation. However, the limited partnership points vary a little whereby the investor liability is limited to the amount agreed upon as the investment capital share of the partner.

In most cases, the limited partnership function is only that of providing additional funds for the business without having any say in the daily running of said business entity. The advantages of this type of partnership would include the retaining of complete control by the original general partner and the limited investment would equal limited liability incurred if any.

It's also an easy way to secure additional capital without the hassle of extensive documentation and there are no direct taxation conforming requirements. Therefore with these options to choose from the individual has to decide which one is best for the business expansion and for the individual personal preference. A partnership structure can make sense if you're going into business with a trusted friend or family member. It's simple to set up, but generally each partner has unlimited personal liability for any debts or obligations incurred by the partnership.

Limited Liability Company

The "Limited Liability Company," or LLC, is a corporate-type business organizational structure that is idea for small businesses and companies, combining as it does the advantages of Sole Proprietorship with the protection and tax advantages of organizing. An LLC can consist of one person which is often the case. As an LLC, your personal assets are separate from those of the business, and therefore protected from loss in case the business should be sued for any reason.

A limited liability company, or LLC, is similar to a partnership but has the legal protections of personal assets that a corporation offers without the burdensome formalities, paperwork and fees. The exact rules for forming an LLC vary by state. Even though most states don't require any annual paperwork or administrative procedures, you should document major business proceedings and lay out some formal procedures — like one meeting a year — to help protect your LLC status.

Additionally, an LLC is not taxed unless it chooses to be (see below); typically, you will pay Self-Employment tax on any profits you take out of the business. The advantages of a Limited Liability Company: No board of directors or shareholder meetings are required; an LLC can consist of just one person. An LLC is an enduring entity, usually separate from the member(s), and can be passed on, transferred or sold; fewer legal complications result should the owner unexpectedly die. Administrative paperwork and recordkeeping is easier.

Your assets are separate from those of the business, therefore you are not liable for damages caused, or debts incurred by the LLC. Taxation is typically on profits taken out by you, not on the LLC. You may however elect to be taxed as a sole proprietor, an S-Corp or a "regular" C- corporation; your tax advisor can determine what is best for your particular situation.

Disadvantages of a Limited Liability Company: Several states levy a franchise tax on LLCs. This is essentially a fee paid for the privilege of shielding one's personal assets. It is more difficult to raise capital, since most investors are looking toward an eventual initial public offering of stock. Any income you receive from an LLC is taxed at "ordinary income" rates, and is subject to FICA taxes (unlike dividend or share income).

Some states charge annual fees and taxes that can diminish the economic advantage of choosing to become an LLC. Among LLC advantages: pass-through taxation – meaning the profits and losses "pass through," the business to the individuals owning the business who report this information on their own personal tax returns. The result can be paying less in taxes, since profits are not taxed at both the business level and the personal level. Another plus: Owners aren't usually responsible for the company's debts and liabilities.

Beyond the fact that forming an LLC is a one-step process requiring little in the way of red tape, you won't have to worry about annual meetings and keeping minutes of those meetings in the way corporations must do. Dividends of S- Corporations must be distributed among shareholders based on the number of shares they hold, regardless of whether or not they contributed to the business in any tangible way, (in other words, YOU could put in the hours of actual labor while THEY sit around the pool waiting for the dividend check – which in theory, could mean your shareholders may wind up with the lion's share of profits)! With an LLC, profits and losses are divided up among the members in any way they see fit. Finally, an LLC can be owned and operated by anyone, whether they are a citizen, a resident alien, or another person or corporate/business entity inside or outside of the U.S.

In the alternative, an S-Corporation, on the other hand must be owned by a "natural person" who is a U.S. citizen or a legal resident – it cannot be owned by another corporation or person outside of the country. Members of an S-Corporation pay Medicare and Social Security taxes only on money they actually receive as compensation in the form of wages or a salary – profits received as a dividend are exempt. In contrast, members of an LLC may be liable for these taxes on all profits made. This is especially true if yours is an online business that provides professional services in the fields of health care, the law or engineering and design. If this is the case for you, it's a good idea to consult with your accountant or tax advisor on what is best for your business.

Another caveat for licensed professionals residing in the State of California: an LLC may not even be an option for you, since California law prohibits LLCs from rendering professional services as an individual. Other than that, California charges LLCs a yearly tax of $800 just for doing business in that state, plus an additional annual LLC fee based on a percentage of total yearly income from all sources.

Lastly, once you've decided to incorporate, where should you do it? This is no small question, since the Internet has made boundaries between states – and even nations – a lot more permeable than they once were, especially when it comes to commerce.

The "Limited Liability Company," or LLC, is a corporate-type business organizational structure that is ideal for small businesses and companies, combining as it does the advantages of Sole Proprietorship with the protection and tax advantages of incorporation. An LLC can consist of one person which is very likely your case, if you are operating an online business. As an LLC, your personal assets are separate from those of the business, and therefore protected from loss in case the business should be sued for any reason. In addition, an LLC is not taxed unless it chooses to be (see below); typically, you will pay Self-Employment tax on any profits you take out of the business.

The advantages of a Limited Liability Company: No board of directors or shareholder meetings are required; an LLC can consist of just one person. An LLC is an enduring entity, usually separate from the member(s), and can be passed on, transferred or sold; fewer legal complications result should the owner unexpectedly die. Administrative paperwork and recordkeeping is easier. Your assets are separate from those of the business, therefore you are not liable for damages caused, or debts incurred by the LLC. Taxation is typically on profits taken out by you, not on the LLC. You may however elect to be taxed as a sole proprietor, an S-Corp or a "regular" C- corporation; your tax advisor can determine what is best for your particular situation.

Disadvantages of a Limited Liability Company: Several states levy a franchise tax on LLCs. This is essentially a fee paid for the privilege of shielding a person's personal assets. It is more difficult to raise capital, since most investors are looking toward an eventual initial public offering of stock. Any income you receive from an LLC is taxed at "ordinary income" rates, and is subject to FICA taxes (unlike dividend or share income).

Note that last point. Currently, dividends are taxed at a maximum rate of 15%, whereas – depending on the amount wages and salaries are taxed up to 38% and may be subject to an additional, "self-employment tax" of over 15%. In the next chapter, you'll find that there are several types of corporate setups, and not everyone is right for the small, single-person on-line operation.

Corporation

A corporation is, at the most basic level, nothing more than a group of people, (even if it's a group of one), banding together under some type of law or regulation, for the purpose of minimizing risk and protecting assets. You should also know by now that corporations are taxed differently than individuals, enabling the owners to keep more of what they make. Since a corporation exists as a separate entity, it has continuity in the event of the principal's death, and ownership interest can be easily transferred.

The kind of corporation you'll want to form depends on a number of factors. Are you still planning to run your business (whether online or offline) by yourself, with a partner or partners, or will you be hiring employees or contracting with third parties? You may wish to consult with your tax advisor or accountant when considering which kind of corporate entity to form with your business.

C-Corporations

This is the most common kind of corporate entity. Most major companies as well as numerous smaller ones fall into this category. Although widely used, a C-Corp structure may not be the best one for a small net-based business run by one person. The reason is that Federal and most State laws require that the operations of a C-Corporation be overseen by a board of directors and that shareholders be consulted on major business decisions. This Board of Directors manages the corporation and appoints officers to run things on a day- to-day basis.

If you plan to expand your Internet business substantially – if you believe it has a shot at becoming the next Google or Craigslist - a C-Corporation is definitely the way to go. As a C-Corporation, you have no limit to how many shareholders you may have, allowing you to raise unlimited amounts of capital through the sale of stock. A C-Corporation is also able to deduct the cost of employee benefits (such as health insurance) as a cost of doing business. Otherwise, if you plan on staying small and intend to maintain maximum control over as much of the operation of your business as possible, formation of an LLC or an S-Corporation is a better choice.

S-Corporations

An S-Corporation – sometimes called a, "small business corporation" - is really little more than a C-Corporation that has chosen to operate under specific tax laws as outlined under Chapter One, Subchapter S of the Internal Revenue Code. The initial administrative paperwork required is the same, regardless of whether you are forming a C-Corporation or an S-Corporation, since this is done at the state level.

Members of an S-Corporation pay Medicare and Social Security taxes only on money they actually receive as compensation in the form of wages or a salary – profits received as a dividend are exempt. In contrast, members of an LLC may be liable for these taxes on all profits made. This is especially true if yours is an online business that provides professional services in the fields of health care, the law or engineering and design. If this is the case for you, it's a good idea to consult with your account or tax advisor on what is best for your business.

Another caveat for licensed professionals residing in the State of California: an LLC may not even be an option for you, since California law prohibits LLCs from rendering professional services as an individual. Other than that, California charges LLCs a yearly tax of $800 just for doing business in that state, plus an additional annual LLC fee based on a percentage of total yearly income from all sources.

Nonprofit

More people are discovering that there are things in the world to which a monetary price cannot be attached – and the value of which may not necessarily be measurable in dollars and cents. For example, the fine arts – contemporary painting or sculpture, modern classical music, and great theatre are institutions that rarely find any kind of support from commercial markets, (in fact, the technical definition of "classical" music is that which is primarily state-supported – something commonly done in Europe, Japan and China, but almost never in the U.S.).

If you are among those who aspire to create a charitable enterprise, such as a patron of the arts, a Nonprofit entity may be for you. Also called a "Not-for profit corporation," a Non-Profit is a non-stock entity (in other words, it cannot issue stock to shareholders), that as the name implies, is not intended to make profits. Such corporations are founded with a specific goal or purpose in mind, usually – but not necessarily – related to education, charity work or the arts. As such, they may be – and often are – exempt from many taxes and tax regulations.

A Nonprofit may certainly generate income, and indeed needs to do so in order to stay in operation. It can accept, hold and trade monetary instruments as well as tangible goods, and – despite the name – can legally make a profit – technically called "revenue" - on such transactions. The use of such revenue – and how much revenue can be made legally - is subject to scrutiny, however, and is tightly regulated. Since it has "members" (like an LLC) rather than "shareholders" or "stockholders," capital is generally raised by soliciting donations from the public, or from private industries. Depending on the purpose of your Non-Profit organization, such donations may be tax-deductible for the donor.

Another major advantage to having a non-profit corporation – especially in the arts – is the ability to apply for government grants, such as those offered by the National Endowment for the Arts (NEA). In 1995, the new Congress changed numerous laws, making these grants unavailable to individuals. However, a non-profit organization can apply for these grants on behalf of individuals, should they wish to commission a work of art.

The same is true of charitable and educational organizations. Numerous Federal and State grants are available to non-profit organizations that cannot be applied for any other way. So – what is your passion? The arts? Education? Providing affordable housing to low-income people? Historical preservation? There are even non-profit sports organizations. You won't get rich, but by incorporating as a non-profit entity, chances are good that you'll be able to pursue activities that nourish your soul while retaining the ability to pay the bills.

PLAN YOUR SUCCESS

Putting a business together takes time and patience. Do not try to put it together too quickly. You want to be focused and organized, as this will help you to be "well planned." A business with a strong plan is more likely to succeed than something you just threw together in an hour.

The business plan needs to meet certain criteria; especially if this is a business you need a grant for or a small loan. Banks and agencies that approve grants want to see a solid plan before they take the risk to lend or give you money. It is the same thing when you or anyone else will invest in a company. You want to see their annual report, which gives you this information and more.

As you prepare your business plan, think about what your strengths really are. Is it planning the business, giving creative ideas, or being the solutions finder? Maybe your strength is marketing, but whatever your strengths are, put them to work for you. Work on the strengths first and when you have mastered one, then you can move on to another. Otherwise, it will take you much longer to get things running smoothly.

Below I am going to list different sections of the business plan and explain a little bit about each section. The more you know about the business plan, the better prepared you will be. Remember, if you want to start a business without experience, this is where you can learn much of the information you will need to get started. So let us move forward.

Not all business plans are created equal, but you will at least have basic information to include. Once you begin your plan, it will change over time based on what you find does and doesn't work for you. As you grow your business, you will find that certain things you didn't initially include should be included based on the political leanings and guiding and legal precedent governing your business. If you are not the type of person who likes to drill down to the nitty-gritty of business specifics, I suggest you outsource this project to someone who does. Whether you decide to create your own business plan or not, below are some sections you will want to include.

Executive Summary

The executive summary will tell the person reading the plan what you want for your business. A big mistake often made is burying this information somewhere else in the plan. The summary needs to explain certain things from the start so you need to be clear and concise in the very beginning.

Keep the summary short and businesslike and no more than half of a page. Depending on how complicated or detailed you need to be about how you will use your funds may make the summary a bit longer. As a general rule of thumb however, and since you are just starting out, you only need your summary to be half of a page.

There are some other key elements that need to be included in the plan. They are as follows: business concept, financial features, financial requirements, current business position, and major achievements. These are not the ones I will focus on too much, but just something to keep in mind.

Business Description

Not to be confused with the executive summary, you usually begin this section with a short description of the industry. So this is not really beginning with just your business, but rather how the industry plays a role in your business.

You will want to describe the industry and discuss the outlook and future possibilities of what will go on. This is all gathered from what happened in the past, so it is a prediction of what could happen or is most likely to happen because of business trends. Also, provide information about all the various markets within the industry.

So what you want to talk about is new products and developments that will benefit or affect your business in a positive way. Make sure to get the most reliable data for this part and always list your sources. I'll talk more about sources later in this chapter, as they are important, but I want the focus to be on the different sections of the plan first.

How you will Profit

The main reason for having a business is to make a profit. All businesspersons need to ask themselves, "How do I make money?" When you ask this question, it should open your mind and help you realize the different ways to bring in income. You do not need a huge section just on this topic, but you want to explain factors, which you think will make you successful in making money.

Before presenting the business plan, you want to explain any equity and debt the business will incur and also explain how this will help make your business more profitable. Also include ways you want to expand your business or make it grow using the equity or debt. As an Internet marketer, you probably will not incur much debt or any at all. It depends solely on what you need to get started.

Defining your Market Strategies

Marketing strategies are based on a thorough study of the market. This will help you become very familiar with all parts of the market, including the target market. Defining who your target market is will be very important so you can earn your share of the sales.

When you are defining your market strategies, you will need to, at some point, determine the pricing of your products and or services. A market analysis will help you to determine the pricing. It is also important to know how you compare to your competition and if you can beat them in pricing or not.

Market Share Projection

As mentioned earlier, when you are describing your industry of choice, you want to discuss the outlook and future possibilities. This information will be gathered on past happenings. So your projections are based on what happened previously in the industry.

Believe it or not, your market share projection is also based on your competition as well as promotional strategies. You can look at how much advertising is done, how it is done, and also research how much it will cost you to advertise the same way. You can always come up with different ways to advertise, but you need a benchmark to start out from.

Position of the Business

When talking about your marketing strategy, you will find it is impossible not to talk about the position of your business. What motivates your target and what they require will affect your company's position in the market. Again, there are more questions that need to be asked and answered to understand this better.

A few questions to ask are: how are your competitors positioning themselves? What specific attributes do your products and services have that the competition does not have? What needs does your product fulfill for the customer? After you answer these basic questions, you can then begin to develop your business' position in the market and write about it on the plan.

Pricing

I've touched a little about pricing earlier, but now I want to give you more detail. The price tag you place on your items, whether it is a product or service, will directly affect the success of your business. Strategies for pricing can be very complex, however, the rules are very basic and straightforward.

You must be able to cover costs, lowering costs will lower sales prices, and prices must reflect changes in the market and respond to the demand of your market. Prices must also be established to help assure sales. The longevity of your products, utility, and maintenance must be reviewed on a regular basis and adjust the prices according to the market.

Prices are used to keep the market in order, so this is the last, but not least important strategy to keep in mind when determining your prices. You do not want to just slap a price tag on something because you think people will buy it for the value of it. You have to be in competition with other businesses and play the game strategically.

Distribution

This part is for you, mainly if you are selling physical goods. Since there are many of you out there that may sell goods on eBay or your own website or blog, this is why I need to talk about this section. So what is distribution exactly? It is the entire process of when a product is manufactured to when it is in the hands of the end user – the customer. There are different channels that make up distribution.

Having a strong distribution of products definitely helps you get an edge in your share of the market. The fast the products can go from production to the customer the better. Make sure the products are of quality though because you do not want the customer constantly returning the goods.

Promotional Planning

Advertisements of any kind are all included in the promotional planning. How you distribute the communication about your business is also part of it. The way in which this is designed will result in attracting the right people to do business with.

Some other things that you may not be aware of that are part of promoting your business is how you package your products. Public relations are also included here. Most of the things you are familiar with are advertising, sales promotions, and personal sales. Each strategy is different in its own respect, but very important in the final outcome of the promotion.

Potential Sales

After thoroughly analyzing the market, you need to make a determination using a quantitative outlook, which concerns your business potential. An initial projection in your plan must be formed based on the position of the product, price, distribution, (for physical goods), sales strategies, and how the market is defined.

Competition Analysis

You first need to identify who your competition is. Gather a list of companies that sell the same products or ones that are very similar. For this section, you will make a statement of your business strategy and how it relates to your competition. The main purpose of this part is to pinpoint the strengths and weaknesses of your competition. Knowing this will only help you improve the weaknesses for your own sake.

S.W.O.T. Analysis

A S.W.O.T. analysis is very important for developing your business and keeps it running to its full potential. For those of you who are not familiar with what this is, "S" stands for strengths, "W" is for weaknesses, "O" is for opportunities, and "T" is for Threats. You not only need to learn about the strengths and weaknesses of your competition as you do with competitive analysis, but you also have to realize your own.

The opportunities and threats are more directly related to your competition. You can look at it as the opportunity you have in the midst of all the competition and what it is about your competition that can be a threat to your own place in the market.

Design Plan

Investors need a description of your company's product design and also its development. Within the section, there needs to be a chart showing the development of the product or service. You will also need to include a budget showing how the company will reach goals.

Product and or Service Development Goals

If you are selling physical products, you will need to list the goals here. You can also list the strategies involved for reaching certain goals for a service business. Your goals should be centered on technical and marketing aspects of your products and or services. You need this as an outline for your business partners, or for yourself if you are a sole proprietor, so you know how to work on things to reach your goals.

Budget

Budgets are very important, as you want to make sure you have the funds available to do business in the first place. You also want to have a plan as you make money as to where the money will go in order to help your business grow and to continuously develop and improve it.

If you are designing a product, you need to account for all the costs that will be involved in creating the product, take it to production, and get it to the customer. As for service, you will need to make sure you have the money to get a business plan written, what equipment you may need to help you with your services, and if you need a brick and mortar building to cater to the needs of your clients.

Knowing how each dollar is being spent is very crucial. Proper planning can only help your business while poor planning is very destructive. I have learned that about half of all businesses started will fail within their first year. You can help avoid this with proper budgeting.

Risk Assessment

What risks are involved in either producing products or offering services? During the stages of development of your product or service there will be some risks you need to be aware of. Risks involved with the creation of products usually happen with the technical development of the product. For services, it is usually in the strategies for planning the types of services you offer.

Income Statement

This is a very simple and straightforward report, which shows your business' cash generating abilities. It shows how well your company does in the financial spectrum and is a financial picture of when sales are made and when expenses occur. It helps you better plan for the future of your business as well.

The income statement is a multi-purpose report giving you a bigger picture of how your business is doing overall. Always use this as a guide from year to year and you will get an idea of what changes need to be made.

With your plan you should include a mind map of each component of your business. Search Google® for some sample mind maps. Here you can see all the different components and can add more or take away some as necessary. Having an illustration right before you will help you gather all the ideas possible to set your business up and run it.

Take each section of the mind map at a time and figure out an order to put them in. There is no wrong or right order here, but your instinct may tell you to do certain things before others. Follow that instinct and refer to your resources. This may require more research to see if there is any logical order to implement your business in.

Now take one piece at a time and execute it. Then observe what happens. The parts which work best will require less attention. Now take those pieces which did not deliver an ideal outcome. Focus on them and try to work out a way to improve it. Once it improves, keep executing it. Now repeat this now and for the life of the business.

Note that things will change as your business grows. What worked one time may not work in the future. So always be open to creating new plans for your business. But more importantly, you must be consistent.

FIND FUNDING FOR YOUR START-UP

One key to a successful business start-up and expansion is your ability to obtain and secure appropriate financing. Raising capital is the most basic of all business activities. But, as many new entrepreneurs quickly discover, raising capital may not be easy; in fact, it can be a complex and frustrating process. However, if you are informed and have planned effectively, raising money for your business will not be a painful experience.

There are several sources to consider when looking for financing. It is important to explore all of your options before making a decision. The primary source of capital for most new businesses comes from savings and other forms of personal resources. While credit cards are often used to finance business needs, there may be better options available, even for very small loans. Friends and relatives are also instrumental in helping many entrepreneurs fund their business by offering no or low interest loans. Banks and credit unions will also provide a loan if you can show that your business proposal is sound. And venture capital firms have helped many companies expand in exchange for equity or partial ownership.

Some small business owners have also found success borrowing money and/or creating lines of credit for much needed inventory and merchandise. To ensure success in obtaining the funding, formalize your business operation through the corporation bureau of your state, prepare a well-thought out business plan and provide enough financial documentation to convince the lender that you are a good credit risk. In some instances, you may need to use your personal credit history to guarantee the business loan. However, once you establish your business acumen, establish that you are not a credit risk and build up income history in your business accounts, the lenders will stop looking for your personal credit history.

SBA loan programs are generally intended to encourage longer term small business financing, but actual loan maturities are based on the ability to repay, the purpose of the loan proceeds, and the useful life of the assets financed. However, maximum loan maturities have been established: 25 for real estate; up to 10 years for equipment (depending on the useful life of the equipment); and generally up to seven years for working capital. Short-term loans are also available through the SBA to help small businesses meet their short term and cyclical working capital needs.

Terms of loans may vary from lender to lender, but there are two basic types of loans: short-term and long-term. Generally, a short-term loan has a maturity of up to one year. These include working-capital 1 loans, accounts receivable loans and line of credit. Long-term loans have maturities greater than one year but usually less than seven years. Real estate and equipment loans may have maturities of up to 25 years. Long-term loans are used for major business expenses such as purchasing real estate and facilities, construction, durable equipment, furniture, fixtures, and vehicles.

Approval of your loan request depends on how well you present yourself, your business, and your financial needs to a lender. Remember, lenders want to make loans, but they must make loans they know will be repaid. The best way to improve your chances of obtaining a loan is to prepare a written proposal.

A good loan proposal will contain the following key elements:

1. Business name, names of principals, Social Security number for each principal, and the business address.

2. Purpose of the loan - exactly what the loan will be used for and why it is needed.

3. Amount required - the exact amount you need to achieve your purpose.

4. History and nature of the business - details of what kind of business it is, its age, number of employees and current business assets.

5. Ownership structure - details on your company's legal structure.

6. A Management Profile on each principal in your business.

You will also need financial statements for the past three years which include your business Balance Sheet, Income Statements and Cash Flow Statement. Additionally, you must be willing to pledge collateral as security for the loan just in case your reality doesn't align to your dream. Fortunately or unfortunately, no one will invest in a business wherein the business owners don't invest in. Accordingly, know what you need to do about the facts and figures that feed your business. Additionally, know the numbers behind the numbers to ensure you don't end up on the other side of a Bankruptcy Petition.

MARKET YOUR SERVICES

Whoever said, "build it and they will come," should be sued for false advertising because you can't just set it and forget it and then profit from it. Trust me when I say that there is NOTHING new under the sun because we have more similarities and commonalities that are made manifest when operating a business. Worse yet, there are so many people who offer similar if not the same solutions or services that consumers are confused. And unfortunately confused minds do nothing.

If you fail to differentiate yourself, you will become a business casualty. Or you'll become a, "brokepreneur," wherein you find yourself broke, busted and disgusted despite the brilliance buried within you. Or worse yet, you'll find yourself in the never-ending loop of showing up as a hustlepreneur/parallelpreneur wherein you find yourself expending the best days of your life working for someone else and the rest of your time hustling on the weekend working your business venture.

So instead of operating in the "sea of sameness" wherein people fail to differentiate themselves, you must find a way to show up, step up and stand out amongst the crowd. Find a way to speak to your target/ideal client so that they see you as a superhero that can help them solve a problem that gives them angst or help them live a dream.

For those people whom you want to do business with, these small categories are something you should really pay attention to. There are three categories that you should be mindful of.

Relationship Marketing

Relationship marketing is a fairly new concept as it stands, but in reality, it is something most people learn when they get a job. What you learn is that you should treat the customer so they feel as if they are welcome in the store or company. You want them to feel at home.

This builds a relationship with the very people you want to do business with. Another way to build relationships with people is to remember things about them. When you see them face to face, try and remember their name. When they give you their information send out a birthday, holiday, or anniversary card which can help build a stronger relationship.

This is one marketing category you want to be focused on more than others. The more personable you can be, the better your business will run. Those who are experts in relationship marketing and can relay the importance of this concept can expect to have an easier time growing their coaching business.

Social Marketing

This category has been around, but there are some important ground rules to adhere to. Do a bit of research on the different ways you should market through social media. It is more than just putting an affiliate like on your Facebook wall or on you Twitter feed. You have to engage the audience every way you can and NOT seem like you are just trying to get them to click a link and buy an affiliate offer.

Once you understand the ground rules, the sky is the limit with social marketing. You can join groups and go on message boards, but be warned, you want to build rapport with the members first. There are some places like the "Warrior Forum," that are designed for internet marketers. You still need to build relationships with the members before you dive right in and post your ads.

Content Marketing

Content marketing has been around since the written word. People have been finding ways to communicate with other people since language began. It is something that will not soon die out, so this should be another of your focuses when it comes to marketing.

At the end of the day, you must make your business engaging to attract the person you feel you are called to serve. Attracting people is way more than just speaking in an enthusiastic way and sounding exciting. You have to be authentic as well because people will be able to tell if you are or not. Trust me, if you are just going through the motions, you will not seem real or worse yet, and you will be deemed as a person who is only about making money instead of making a difference.

As previously mentioned in an earlier chapter, you want to attract the right people to your business. Trust me, trying to get as many people as you can to jump on board to be served by you seems like a good idea, but it can cause a lot of problems.

SELLING IS SHARING

Selling is a part of life. Whether you realize it or not, when you go to a job interview, you are "selling" your expertise and skills to the potential employer. People think of sales in a negative connotation, but here is your chance to show people that it is not so bad. Plus people who are already in the sales profession know that they always need to find ways to improve.

More and more people are starting their own businesses, and guess what; sales are going to and always will be a big part of it. How else will you get your clients? Selling is a must, but unlike the old days, the strategies used to sell have changed dramatically.

For this section, I will talk about different selling styles. First selling is not something that can be forced upon others. No matter how you word something, a, "NO" most likely will be a NO. You have to respect that no and realize you do not want to do business with someone who gives you a negative response.

What are some selling styles? Proactive, consultative, aggressive, and passive are some of the styles you may notice. For your business, you may want to take one style and build it all around that. A majority of people will probably want to focus on the passive way of selling. In my life, I have noticed that there are more passive people and introverts than there are impassive people and extroverts.

Now, I want to break these styles down for you and give you a better understanding of each. This is in hopes that if you choose to be a sales coach, you may be able to understand more than one style which in the end will be more profits.

Passive

Passive selling is pretty effective. You do not want to be labeled as a, "pushy salesperson," and so you take this approach. As a coach, you will teach others how to get the sale without "selling to" someone. Passive selling can be achieved in a more laid back setting where people are already aware that your product or service exists.

This makes things easier for you in the long run. Passive selling may require aggressive selling at the start. This is until people are aware of your brand and company. When people become loyal customers, then they will be looking out for new products and services and special offers.

Aggressive

Aggressive is when you seek after people to tell them you have a product and convince them to buy it. As I said above, when your business is new, this may be an approach you need to start with. As more people are aware of your brand, you can transition into a passive approach.

Consultative

This is actually what coaching is about. As a coach, you are not just helping people understand their skills or business better, but rather acting as a type of consultant. You are the expert in your niche, so you can rest assured that there will be people who trust you for your expertise.

Proactive

Proactive selling allows you to cause the sale to happen. You are not just standing to the side, then responding to the sale once a transaction occurred. The sale may never have happened if you were not proactive in it. When you are coaching people with this style, you need to emphasize the importance of being proactive. You are proactive with your sales whether you are passive or aggressive in sales.

Once again, there is no cut and paste, cookie-cutter formula to success. Instead, you must fully appreciate who you are, what exudes naturally from you and the best way to position your solutions and strategies to serve those you feel called to serve. So stop finding some rinse and repeat guidelines. Or an easy way to make money that doesn't feel right to you. Just do you and no other because those assigned to you are waiting for you.

KNOW YOUR NUMBERS

Money is neither good nor bad, but how it is used or misused can affect your personal, professional and business relationships. Unfortunately, many of us have been conditioned to believe that money is evil. In effect, many entrepreneurs fail to study, assess, or track business and/or personal finances.

However to uplevel your business success, you need a system to track the money received. And you need a system to track all of the invoices, expenses, receipts, loans, credit, benefits and passive income. The best way to ensure you keep track of the monies that go in and out of your business is recording financial activities of business.

In order to know your numbers, you must become knowledgeable about financial tools such as Income Statements, Balance Sheet, Debt-to-Income Ratios, Debt Due Date Trackers and Cash Flow Statements.

In brief, the Income Statement tells you where your money came from and where it went. More specifically, a well-documented Income Statement will help you assess what products and/or services makes it most profitable and which might be dissolved.

In contrast, a Balance Sheet gives you an assessment of cash on hand, cash in the bank account, money market accounts, monies owed to others money retained to build a greater legacy. It's worth mentioning that assets also include IOUs and liabilities include any mortgages on assets, credit cards and loans.

A projected Profit and Loss Statement is a review of your month-by month profit and loss account for your net profit (or loss) on a quarterly basis. The Profit and Loss Statement is also a great tool that helps you not only plan how you wish to make money, but also assess whether you are on track of making your monthly, quarterly and yearly goals.

Managing cash flow is key to uplevel your business success. One way to do this is to use one bank account for your business to receive money and to expend money. In so doing, your banker will be better able to determine if you are creditworthy so much so that your bank extends credit to you. If money is extended to your company and you pay back any credit extension on time, your business will be extended more credit which could serve as a life saver.

Knowing your numbers also entails knowing what you need in the future to build a better legacy for later. If you're an author, speaker or coach, you need to start thinking in units (whether books or coaching programs), as it relates to not only your immediate cash flow goals, but your legacy building goals as well. Similarly, if you rent products to consumers, you must consider how many units must be rented to ensure you hit your monthly savings goals.

Thinking beyond your reality may be new to some because of conditioning of surviving life instead of thriving in it. However, if you don't think beyond your realities, you will always find yourself with barely enough or worse yet, hustling for life. During your healthy years, you must focus on short-term and long-term personal and business goals. In addition, you must focus on legacy building goals to ensure that you have a nice amount of money saved for when you decide to do something different.

You must consistently take action to connect, engage and serve your client and/or customer with a product or service that reflects the brilliance of you. You must also ensure that you continually create more than you consume to ensure you have more assets than liabilities. And you must consistently ensure that your money ultimately works for you by investing in programs and services that helps you reach your legacy building goals so that you don't have to hustle all of your life.

PROTECT YOUR ASSETS

In naming your business it is important not to violate trademark laws. This means not naming your website in a way that might create a "likelihood of confusion" with a preexisting commercial enterprise in the same field.

Such confusion might arise if the name you choose is identical or very similar to the name of another business or product. So before you settle for a name, hire a graphic designer, put a TM on your name or anything else you heard to do from your friends, associates, accountants and business coaches (wink-wink), you may want to take the time to seek to know if anyone else has a trademark that is close, equivalent or using what you thought was unique to you.

Maintain trade secrecy. Stay quiet about your pending patents and intellectual property developments. You don't need to force anyone who enters your office into signing a non-disclosure agreement (NDA), but you do need to maintain a controlled system of information flow that allows development detail to filter down only to those who actually need to know. Sensitive information should be kept secret until you have a patent pending or in effect.

Enforce formal ownership agreements for intellectual property (hereinafter referred to as "IP"). Create a formal contract agreement among you, your product developers, and other founders or partners of your business venture. Ensure that a clear agreement exists on who gets what ownership stakes in any pending patents and how intellectual property will be divided among all those included. Furthermore, enforce clear contractual claims on any pending IP or patents so that your developers can't later claim partial ownership without prior agreement.

A non-compete agreement is a little different from an non-disclosure agreement (also referred to as an NDA). A non-compete agreement essentially states that the person working for you is not allowed to compete with you or work for your competitors for a certain number of years after leaving your employ. These are typically meant for full-time employees. They are not usually meant for people who do contract work, because it would prevent them from making a living after their work with you is finished.

The next three chapters will go more in depth into patents, trademarks and copyrights to help you appreciate why you need them and when you need them. In some instances, you need all three, but for most savvy CEOpreneurs, you only need a few based on what you create (or have created) for you.

PATENT YOUR PRODUCTS

Businesses and individuals undertaking commercial endeavors create and deal with intellectual property rights such as patents and trademarks. For persons and entities engaged in trade, obtaining, maintaining and protecting property rights such as patents and trademarks can give a competitive edge in the marketplace. Patents grant the holder the exclusive right to an invention such as a mechanical process, composition or design.

The applicant for a patent must be the inventor or the inventor's legal representative, (such as a guardian, heir, estate administrator or executor, or lawyer). When an invention is made by two or more persons jointly, they must apply jointly for the patent. Inventors may apply for a patent jointly even though (1) they did not physically work together or at the same time, (2) each did not make the same type or amount of contribution, or (3) each did not make a contribution to the subject matter of every claim of the patent.

If a joint inventor refuses to join in an application for a patent or cannot be found or reached after diligent effort, the application may be made by the other inventor on behalf of himself and the omitted inventor. It is important to knowingly designate the true inventor(s) for any willful deception in naming the inventors can lead to an invalidation of any subsequent patent that issues. If the wrong individual is unknowingly listed as the inventor or one of the inventors, the USPTO will permit an amendment of the application to correct the error. The inventor does not need to be a United States Citizen to apply for a U.S. Patent.

In order for an invention to be patentable it must be novel (i.e. new) and non-obvious. Under federal law, the USPTO will reject a patent as not being novel if, "(a) the invention was known or used previously by others in this country, or previously patented or described in a printed publication in this or a foreign country," or "(b) the invention was patented or described in a printed publication in this or a foreign country or in public use or on sale in this country more than one year prior to the application for patent in the United States." This means that even if the inventor published his patent himself in a foreign or U.S. publication, he must apply for a U.S. patent within one year of that publication or his application will be denied as not being novel.

The non-obvious requirement means that, "a patent may not be obtained even though the invention is not identically disclosed or described in another publication, if the differences between the subject matter sought to be patented and the published patent are such that the subject matter as a whole would have been obvious at the time the invention was made to a person having ordinary skill in the field of science or "art" that relates to the patent."

Under federal patent law, in order to be patentable, the invention must be useful in the sense of purpose as well as in the sense of mechanical functionality. Of note is that pursuant to the Atomic Energy Act of 1954, if the invention is only useful in the, "utilization of special nuclear material or atomic energy for atomic weapons," then a patent will not issue.

Since patents will only be granted to novel, nonobvious and useful inventions that have not been published before, it is better practice for the applicant to conduct a search of patents before completing an application. While patent attorneys and agents will conduct such a search, applicants can conduct their own searched at the USPTO website, by going to the Patent Search Room in Virginia or by going to a Patent and Trademark Depository Library (PTDL). The USPTO's Official Gazette as well as website has a listing of PTDLs in each state.

TRADEMARK YOUR BRAND

Trademarks, as the term is generally used, are distinctive names, logos, designs, numbers, symbols, or signs that are used to identify and distinguish the source of a particular product or service. The property right that is represented by and embodied in a trademark is termed goodwill. Goodwill is in general the association in the public mind between the mark, the provider of particular goods and/or services and the quality of the particular goods and/or services sold. Examples of trademarks with Goodwill are Microsoft, NBA, and RCA. Goodwill is created by the actual use of the mark in commerce and advertising of the mark. From this basic principal develops the legal fact that the person or entity that uses a mark in commerce first has the greatest, and at times sole right to use that mark.

Of note is that the more fanciful and arbitrary the mark, the greater the goodwill in the mark and therefore the greater the likelihood that the United States Patent and Trademark Office ("USPTO") will register the mark. The USPTO generally will not register marks that are descriptive or misdescriptive of the goods/services, geographically descriptive or misdescriptive of the goods/services, a surname or ornamental. There are other grounds on which the USPTO will reject registration and these are set forth in the USPTO's Trademark Manual of Examining Procedure (TMEP) in Chapter 1200. (See also 15 U.S.C. §1052).

Federal registration of a mark is not required as it does not grant the right to use the mark in commerce nor does it create goodwill in the mark. The owner already has the right to use a mark in commerce and can only create goodwill by using and/or advertising the mark. Federal registration of a mark instead gives the owner in the eyes of the U.S. federal government and courts the presumption that he/she has the sole right to prevent others from using a confusingly similar mark in commerce in any of the 52 U.S. states and U.S. possessions.

Federal registration also provides the owner with the right to 1) bring an infringement or dilution action in U.S. federal court, 2) to prevent third parties from importing similar/ the same goods or services into the U.S. under a confusingly similar or counterfeit mark by registering the mark with the U.S. Customs Service, and 3) use the U.S registration as a basis to register the same mark internationally (See 15 U.S.C. §1051). Of note, is that the registration of a mark does not permit the owner to prevent others from making the same goods or from selling the same goods or services under a clearly different mark.

Trademarks, like brands, build strength over time. The test for trademark infringement is "confusing similarity." Put another way, if the average consumer believes both products to have come from the same source, there is infringement. Obviously, the more a consumer is familiar with a particular brand, the more defendable its mark.

That's why it behooves a company to do the following: Choose a distinctive mark, including a "coined" name. Brand names range from generic and descriptive to suggestive and arbitrary or fanciful ("coined"). Obviously it takes longer to build meaning for coined names, but they are also more distinctive and easiest to protect legally. Kodak, Xerox, and Exxon fall in that category.

Suggestive marks are the next most protectable. Examples include Coppertone, Duracell, and Listerine. Even common words can be used as trademarks as long as they are not used descriptively. These common words/phrases are also suggestive marks: Amazon (big), Twitter (brief and chatty), and Apple (different, offbeat). Descriptive marks are not protectable unless the brand creates a secondary meaning for the word, such as Weight Watchers, Rollerblade, or White-Out. Generic marks, such as Shredded Wheat and Super Glue, are not protectable at all.

Avoid geographic names as a part of your mark—they can be the basis of trademark refusal. Register the mark. Be consistent in the use of the mark. Create strong trade dress, (as discussed later in this chapter). Widely advertise and distribute its trademarked products.

Because the strength of a mark is dependent upon consumers' familiarity with it, it is much easier for a competitor to neutralize your mark soon after it has been introduced than after it has been in use for a long period of time. Courts use the following tests to determine infringement. Strength of the trademark claiming infringement. Similarity of the two marks. Evidence of consumer confusion. Care a consumer takes in comparing products. Intent of the organization in using the potentially infringing mark.

By using the mark in association with your products and services over time, you gain trademark protection. Registering your mark, (marks can be registered at the state and federal levels), provides additional protection. Although common law and federal trademark statute protect an unregistered mark, registering your mark transfers the burden of proof to the second comer in challenging a mark's registration. With federal registration, you can sue infringers in federal court. Also, after five years of registration, the mark becomes incontestable. Federal trademark registrations last ten years and can be renewed every ten years ad infinitum.

You can acquire trademark rights in one of two ways. To acquire trademark rights based on use in commerce, you must be the first person or organization that uses the mark in conjunction with the products or services for which trademark protection is sought. To acquire the mark base on intent to use, you must apply to register the mark through the United States Patent and Trademark Office (uspto.gov).

Before choosing a trademark, first conduct a simple search to eliminate marks that are not available. This search can be done online for free. After that, for the remaining candidates, conduct a full search through a law firm specializing in trademark law or through an experienced trademark search firm.

Strong brands run the danger of becoming category descriptors. Always use trademarks as adjectives, not verbs or nouns. If your brand is in danger of becoming a category descriptor, consider talking about your brand in the following way that differentiates the brand from the category. For example: "Jell-O® gelatin," "Kleenex® facial tissue," and "Xerox® photocopier."

In naming your business it is important not to violate trademark laws. This means not naming your website in a way that might create a "likelihood of confusion" with a preexisting commercial enterprise in the same field. Such confusion might arise if the name you choose is identical or very similar to the name of another business or product.

COPYRIGHT YOUR CREATIVE WORKS

A big part of establishing your reputation vis-à-vis clients and the public lies in promoting yourself as an expert in your field. In some cases, that might mean distribution of written information such as blog posts, website content, guides, instructions, and information packages that demonstrate your expertise. Accordingly, registering your creative works should be one of your standard operating procedures.

Without a registered copyright, you must police, prove and pay handsomely to protect your books, keynotes, poems, curriculum, music, lyrics, photos and everything else your creative mind creates throughout your lifetime. If you don't believe copyrighting your products is worthy of the cost of doing business, just take a look at the litigation wherein creative geniuses are receiving masses of money from imitators, duplicators and violators.

A copyright is a form of protection provided by the laws of the United States to authors of, "original works of authorship." This includes literary, dramatic, musical, artistic and certain other creative works. The advantages of registering a copyright at copyright.gov include the following:

1. Establishes a public record of the copyright holder's ownership.

2. Enables copyright holders to sue infringers in federal court. The first thing you need is a copyright. Copyrights are used on websites and in products – and may even be used in emails. Many people

mistakenly think that copyrighting information requires filling out forms and paying fees. This isn't true. The fact is that as soon as you write something down or create something, it is copyrighted. You don't ever have to fill out a form, or pay a copyright fee, although in some instances, you may want to. This is typically done for hard copy books, music, and other creatives – but not usually done for digital products. This doesn't mean that it cannot be done for digital products.

The fastest way to copyright something, however, is to add this statement:

Copyright © YEAR by Your Company Name All Rights Reserved.

That alone takes care of it, although because the person who first writes or creates something owns the copyright, it is important that you have some documentation that indicates the exact date that the product was created, in case someone tries to infringe on your copyright.

If you have work created for you, it is called, 'work for hire.' Usually, the law requires that the copyright is automatically transferred to the person paying for the work, when the creator is paid for that work. However, depending on whom you are dealing with, you may want to create an agreement that states exactly when and how the copyright is transferred to you.

Of course, copyrighting work doesn't necessarily prevent others from stealing your hard work. There are many out there who are not above plagiarism – and this is a problem.

It's unlikely that you will capture everyone who controls, alts and uploads your brilliance as their own, but there are a few resources that may help you police your creative works. First, there is Copyscape.com, a free service. Copyscape allows you to see if others are using your work without giving you credit. Second, you can create a Non-Disclosure Agreement wherein you request that anyone receiving your information does not disclose it to others. Third, you can create a Non-Compete Agreement wherein you require by agreement that those working with you as you build your empire don't turn around and use your intellectual property as their own.

You can find many samples of non-disclosure agreements; just make sure the language is specific to what you actually want to protect. Otherwise it's a waste of time should you need to file a lawsuit to preclude an imitator or duplicator from monetizing from your brilliance without an agreement. As an added precaution, have agreements signed and notarized to avoid any false claims of 'not knowing,' 'not violating' and/or 'not executing' any agreements.

PUT IT IN WRITING

There's nothing that beats conversation like documentation! I have this one client, his agreement was just to do security work, wiring. All he was supposed to do was wiring. The next thing you know, someone found out that he did DJ work and they're like, "Well, we want you to do this and we want you to do that." And I was like, "Did you negotiate those agreements?"

Unfortunately, he did not have that in place and he just felt obligated to do the work. If he had an agreement in place, my client could have pinpointed the terms of the agreement and determined whether or not he wanted to do additional work. In the alternative, he could have had a clause in the contract or service agreement wherein his client would have been told in advance what additional work would cost. Unfortunately, when terms are not put in writing, it can cause confusion, chaos or calamity when the other party makes demands outside of the original agreement.

In another instance, a client had a contract in place, but it didn't address the issue of whether or not the contract was assignable. In an unrelated scenario, a commercial cleaning contractor had an agreement with a building manager to supply cleaning services. For years, the contract was renewed automatically as the parties to the contract liked, knew and respected one another. Then one day, the service provider learned that the building was sold and the owner assigned the contract to the new owner.

When the business closed down and someone else bought the building and they went to her and said, "Oh, we had this agreement from this other person and we're going to utilize your service." Well, she wanted to renegotiate her contract and they're like, "No, we bought the terms and the conditions and we bought everything including your cleaning services agreement." She pretty much was stuck because she did not have the requisite language to protect her interests. So she finished the contract with gritted teeth to ensure you didn't get sued for voiding the contract.

I hope you learn the requisite lessons which is to be specific about the terms of your agreement. This lesson is especially pertinent when hiring independent contractors to complete specialized work or provide temporary help is becoming more common every day. It doesn't matter if a company is small or large, local or international, or anything in between, many use contractors to Design, Web development, Write Articles, Virtual Assistant Services, Marketing and public relations, Video, photo and audio services, Software development, Search marketing, Translation services and Social media support.

Accordingly, you must be strategic about protecting your business with agreements. Each freelancer you hire to complete a project or task for you should sign an independent contractor agreement, and this includes your friends and family members! In being the boss of your business, you must learn to delegate to others; especially wise legal counsel who can help you mitigate damages of working with others... especially unscrupulous individuals.

Every business enters into contracts. Most businesses actually enter into contracts every day, for example a contract with each customer. Many contracts are verbal, or entered into by email. It can be difficult to be sure what you've agreed to.

It's important that business contracts are set out in writing, to protect you and the customer. It's wise to set up standard contracts, so it's very easy to provide a written contract quickly. For example, your business can have standard sales terms and conditions, a standard employment agreement, standard contractor agreement and a standard license agreement.

A contract is usually structured with the operative, or business-specific clauses, at the beginning of the document. The more standard "boilerplate" clauses, that address general legal issues, are generally at the end. Generally the majority of the time spent drafting or reviewing and negotiating a contract will be spent on the operative or business-specific clauses.

You can work out and negotiate the economic and business specific details before you bring in your lawyer. The lawyers can then negotiate the finer details of the contract without spending time on the business specific issues.

Finally, it's important that you work with a lawyer who has specific experience either drafting or reviewing the contract in question. A franchise lawyer should draft or review a franchise agreement. A lawyer with expertise in commercial leasing should assist you with your commercial leasing needs.

Even if you don't retain, an attorney, ensure your contracts have the following information:

1. Parties and verified addresses, EIN or social security number.

2. A specific description of the payment terms and when payment will be made.

3. Equipment, Supplies, and Materials

4. Out-of-Pocket Expenses

5. Independent Contractor Relationship

6. State and Federal Income Taxes

7. Permits, Licenses, and Liability Insurance

8. Termination and Disputes

9. Intellectual Property

10. Indemnification

Always remember, NOTHING beats communication like documentation. So even if you trust someone, be the boss of your business by ensuring all of your agreements are in writing.

SUCCESSION BUSINESS PLANNING

As a business owner, you have a lot of responsibilities resting on your shoulders. From your family to your clients, employees, and partners, there are a lot of people counting on you today and in the future. Do you have a business succession plan in place to make sure they're all taken care of if you can no longer take care of your business?

Unfortunately, most businesses aren't liquid enough to continue operating and supporting the owner's family and employees if the owner dies or is no longer physically or mentally capable of running the company. However, with the right plan in place, you can ensure the people you care about the most are well provided for if anything happens to you.

In other words, you need a life and death plan that fully, (and correctly), identifies what should happen to your business if you can't run it anymore. I know, thinking about your death isn't the most pleasant prospect, but doing so can actually make both your life and your business so much better.

The truth is you need a business succession plan that ensures the people you care about avoid facing true disasters when you're gone. For example, here are just five of the disasters waiting in the future if you don't have a rock solid business succession plan in place before you die or become unable to run your business:

1. Your business will have to close because you don't have enough insurance, (or the right kind of insurance), to provide the cash needed to keep the business going.

2. Someone you don't want to lead your company could end up in charge if you don't have a written plan in place that designates who will run your business, (or prepare it for sale).

3. Your business won't be able to serve its customers, collect payments, or pay bills because there is no documented access to your digital business assets.

4. Your business and your family will have to fight to keep your business if they end up in probate court.

5. Your business and personal assets as well as your intellectual property could be lost to the State Department of Unclaimed Property.

The good news is that all of these disasters are easily avoided with a well-written business succession plan. Once you have this plan in place, you'll have peace of mind that if anything happens to you, the people you care about most—your family, clients, team, and partners—will be cared for in exactly the way that you want. This reassurance frees you up to focus on generating more income and making your big dreams a reality today!

When you create and document your business succession plan, you not only ensure the operational legacy of your business is protected, but you can also secure the more personal legacy of your business. Through written, video, and audio recordings, you can save the story of your business and leave a documented legacy of your experiences and the lessons you learned along the way as you built a successful company. It's an important part of business succession planning that you shouldn't forget!

Additionally, your family needs direction regarding key people, key contracts, property and what happens if and when you cannot make your side of the bargain. Unfortunately, without direction, the wrong person could take your heart work and run it into the ground through Intestate Succession. Or worse yet, your family would be unaware of the day-to-day operations of your business so much so that they don't have the necessary information to continue the business as you would.

Accordingly, it is advisable that you take the time from your busy schedule to ensure that Guardianship is in place should you have minor children. You also need to appoint someone take over your finances and medical decisions by drafting a Power of Attorney that complies with your state. You should also have a will and Living Will drafted to ensure that a health condition, long-term illness or death doesn't stunt your business growth and/or legacy.

DON'T PLAY WITH THE IRS

I've worked with the Internal Revenue Service (IRS), the Securities Exchange Commission (SEC) and the Department of Labor (DOL) and they do not play. In terms of their audits, they have authority to knock on your door and ask questions, send you a letter request for information and/or subpoena you to come into their office to substantiate your claim of abiding by all of the relevant laws in terms of your business operations. And most of the auditors, investigators and inspectors do not care about you. Instead, they care about whether or not you are handling business in compliance of the law.

In order to prepare for any pop-up audits, you must be proactive about learning the rules and regulations, documenting your decisions, keeping your personal and business assets separate and being ready, willing and able to be forthcoming about your business operations.

The IRS will go over your paperwork and will document what you do and don't have. The IRS investigators will also document conversations that you have. Accordingly, when you are under investigation, it's imperative that you remember than you and government agents/investigators are not your friends. To ensure you don't get in trouble with the law, you must work your business like a boss.

When reporting income, report it straight across the board. Report your income, don't play any games wherein sometime you are an employee and other times you are an independent contractor. Don't play around with expense and earnings either because if you're ever audited and can't substantiate your claim of living in a gated community, but only reporting less than minimum wage, you will be deemed as a liar and deceiver. And that is not a good thing.

As I mentioned before, the IRS can randomly knock on your door and request information related to gift substantiation if you are running a nonprofit, entertainment reimbursement, employee benefit plan and/or to assess the profitability of your business ventures. The auditors and investigators are well versed in the law because most are attorneys. Additionally, they have been trained to spot a sham business or an over-reporter.

Don't forget in law enforcement world, they are trained to spot inconsistencies. Do an assessment of your last three reported tax returns to assess whether or not you are consistent in your business operation. If you are not consistent in your operations, you will be flagged as a potential violator of the law. Additionally you need to maintain accurate records.

Keep a binder that houses all of your governing documents, including articles of incorporation, bylaws, constitutions, operating agreements, service agreement and reimbursement policies. In addition, keep track of contracts, payment history, contract cancellations, bad debt reports and bankruptcy filing of your customer.

If you have any distribution, you need to keep track of that. If you have a return policy or not a return policy, you definitely need to keep track of that. Additionally, if you offer coaching programs wherein you collect more than $10,000 from your clients per year, you must file form 8300.

Another thing, if you only have one car, please, please, please be smart about how you are keeping track of your mileage. There's nothing in the rules that says that you have to have two separate cars. The only rule say that you need to have the documents in place due diligence with regards to the documents. It's fabulous that you are using the car, like you said you are using the car for that particular time and place. Similarly, if you are using your home as a business space and you're writing that of like some of us. I don't even write it off because of the specificity regarding measurements where mix-use. And I don't want to set myself up for an audit.

DON'T IGNORE THE FTC

Federal Trade Commission rules regarding e-commerce are constantly changing to keep up with advances in technology. In addition, many existing FTC rules – such as those governing telemarketers – may be applied to e-mail marketing. As a businessperson, you should visit the Federal Trade Commission website periodically for the latest guidelines (http://www.ftc.gov).

What the FTC labels as "unfair or deceptive acts or practices" refers to:

- advertising claims
- marketing and promotional techniques
- general sales practices

These rules are applicable to all forms of communication, from print advertising to live demonstrations. Since the dawn of the Internet Age back around 1994, over 100 legal actions have been taken against online businesses allegedly engaged in "unfair or deceptive acts or practices." FTC issues rules, which are clear prohibitions against these acts, and guidelines, which are examples designed to help online business owners such as yourself in complying with FTC rules.

Fair Play

The three basic principles of advertising law are no doubt familiar to you, but they bear reviewing:

• Ads must be truthful and contain no misleading material

- The advertiser must provide evidence, or "substantiation" of any claims

Whether you write your own ad copy or hire a professional, you should readily be able to identify any claims of product or service benefits and determine if any express (stated) or implied claims might be misconstrued. Any claims that fall into that category require disclosure, or qualifying information.

Disclosures

It may seem unfair to you as an honest merchant or service provider, but legally, you are required to phrase your advertising message in such a way that it absolutely cannot be misconstrued in any way – and failing to do that can leave you or your company liable. Fortunately, compliance is not difficult. A common way to fulfill this obligation is to use disclaimers such as: "Your results may vary," or "not proven to work for all situations." It is however your responsibility to determine (A) which claims may require substantiation, and

(B) what information should be included in any disclosure.

Now, it's important to understand that a disclosure can only qualify a claim or limit it so your potential customer doesn't receive a misleading impression. It's not a license to make a false claim. If a disclosure completely contradicts your claim, that claim is false and requires modification.

Beyond qualifying claims about a given product or service, a disclosure is also required in order to provide your potential client about the terms of the transaction. You'll see good examples of this if and when you start searching online for paralegal help in incorporating your business. The most reputable firms will have a clear statement on at least one of their web pages, (and usually more), that goes something like this: XXXXXXX

No Fine Print

FTC rules require that any disclosures be, "clearly and conspicuously," displayed in an online advertisement. In the old days of early print ads, unscrupulous merchants, service providers and companies used the, "fine print," to get around any disclosure requirements, knowing that few people ever read an entire advertisement.

Just as almost nobody reads every word on a printed page, almost nobody reads every single page on a web site. While it can be argued that consumers have control – and even an obligation to control – what material they're viewing online and in what quantities, the fact is that they're probably not looking for disclosures. They probably aren't even expecting to find them, because frankly, they're searching for an answer to their pain, their problem or their desires. It's human nature to see that which we want to see and find that which we want to find. Therefore, the burden is on you as the advertiser to place disclosures where your potential customers cannot possibly miss them.

Clear and Conspicuous Standard

Unfortunately, there is no "one-size-fits-all" solution here. Some creativity and flexibility is required, and the kind of disclosure necessary is going to depend on the information and how it's presented. Online ads can be text-only, use different kinds of graphics, or even audio and video. The bottom line: disclosures must be crystal clear.

While there are no hard-and-fast rules as to what constitutes "clear and conspicuous disclosure," there are a few guidelines:

• Disclosures should be placed in reasonable proximity to the claim which it is qualifying

• Disclosures should be reasonably prominent (easy to see); this refers not only to placement, but to font and choice of colors (high contrast between background and text colors)

• Other elements of the advertisement should not distract from the disclosure

• If the advertisement is lengthy, consider whether or not a disclosure bears repeating over multiple locations and even pages

• If audio and/or video is used, disclosures should be audible, understandable, and in the case of video, appear long enough to be fully read and understood

• Language used in disclosures should be targeted to the intended audience. For example, if your product or service is aimed at fans of monster truck rallies or the Atlanta Braves, chances are you won't want to use a lot of complex legal terms in any disclosure.

Proximity

The "triggering claim" is the one that calls for an immediate disclosure. The most effective way to do this is to make sure the disclosure is part of any product description.

Another issue to be aware of when it comes to a separate disclosures page is clutter. Avoid "click-away" links, banner ads, images (unless such images are part of the disclosure) and superfluous (i.e., unrelated) text – in other words, anything that could possibly distract the viewer from the contents of the disclosure. Your, "click-through" page is for one purpose only.

Anyone who has spent any time at all on the World Wide Web is aware that there is a mind-boggling plethora of hyperlink styles in use. Some are text, some are graphic, some are underlined, some are not – the list goes on (and on).

However, all successful websites use a single style for all the hyperlinks throughout the site. Which style is used depends on the individual site. What is important is that a single style be used for all hyperlinks throughout your website so that visitors will consistently recognize them as such.

Technological, "bells and whistles" such as frames and scrolling text may be tempting to use, especially if you or your web designer are well versed in the more creative uses of Java scripts. Scrolling text can be especially attention-getting, particularly on an otherwise static webpage.

While there is nothing inherently wrong or illegal with using such techniques for your disclosure, it's inadvisable. The reason is something we referred to earlier, and an issue with which every web designer struggles – you have no control over what browser your visitor is using to view your site.

Ironically, it's almost impossible to discover hard and fast statistics on which users are using which browser. It's safe to assume that at least 90% will be using either Microsoft Internet Explorer – which comes bundled with all Windows operating systems – or Netscape. Still, you have no way of knowing which version of the browser is being employed, or at what resolution. New browser versions come out regularly, and while most people today use 19" monitors, the majority will use the default resolution of whatever browser they may have installed. This may or may not be the optimal resolution for viewing elements such as scrolling text or frames.

"Pop-Up" windows have been a favorite of aggressive advertisers practically since the beginning of e-commerce – and in less than 10 years, quickly wore out their welcome with impatient and (justifiably) irritated Web surfers. They're still used of course, but with the increasing (and understandable) popularity of pop-up blocking software – some of which is integrated right into the browser – they are almost completely ineffective today. For that reason, pop-up windows are not a good choice for displaying required disclosures.

"Pop-unders" have gained in popularity in recent years among advertisers, and so far, there seems to be few ways to stop them. The problem is that they tend to go unnoticed until the Web surfer has ended his or her browsing session and closed the main window. As this pertains to disclosures, it means that your customer in all likelihood will not see any such disclosure until after the sale has been completed. Therefore, "pop-unders" are not a good choice, either.

Laws and regulations pertaining to advertising and marketing practices also change and evolve frequently – especially in response to technology. However, in most cases these laws have always favored the protection of the consumer, and continue to do so. There was a time in the U.S. when receiving a corporate charter obligated the entity in question to serve the public good in some way in exchange for asset protection and immunity from liability. Although this is not currently a requirement, many smaller corporations being formed today are voluntarily adding a component of "social responsibility" to their operations. This may be as simple as providing some type of free service to the community, supporting the local community by favoring local and domestic industries in business-to-business transactions, engaging in fair and sustainable trade practices, investing in employees, and more.

LEGALIZE YOUR MARKETING STRATEGIES

An entire volume could be dedicated to the subject of disclosures and all the different ways they might be presented, how to ensure they get attention, and more. While there is no way to be 100% sure your disclosure(s) will be noticed and read, the general rule of thumb is K.I.S.S. (Keep It Simple, Solopreneur). By studying the above examples and combining creative thinking with good study and analysis of your website as to which pages are getting the hits and how traffic flows through your site, you can be almost 100% certain that your disclosure messages are receiving the required attention.

Although it may seem self-evident, it should nonetheless be pointed out that the requirements for disclosures also apply to any expressed warranties as well as terms of sale (i.e. return/refund policies). These are typically hyperlinked – in which case, they need to be prominent and clearly labeled for what they are. In addition, they need to be viewable prior to sale and have "printer-friendly" options. The reason of course is to give the customer access to this material while making the decision to buy, or while comparison shopping.

These guidelines are also extremely important if you run some type of subscription service with a "negative option plan" – in other words, you're going to continue to charge their credit card or other payment account until the buyer notifies you in writing to discontinue. In this case, you have a legal obligation to notify in writing up front and prior to initial sale of such conditions that include:

A) the amount of the recurring charge

B) the monthly date of the recurring charge

C) the procedure and conditions for discontinuing

Additionally, e-mail communication should be used each month to remind the customer of the impending charge, identifying your company, what merchandise or subscription is being shipped or charged for, and when the customer can expect to receive the merchandise or be able to access their subscription. You will need to put this information into the subject heading; additionally, you may need to advise your customers on your site to adjust any "spam" filters they may have so your notices do not get routed to a "bulk mail" folder and disregarded.

Direct Marketing.   Direct marketing refers to a range of targeting advertising techniques. In the "old" (pre-Internet) days, direct marketing techniques consisted primarily of direct mail, (the "junk mail" that clogs your inbox) and telemarketing.

Targeted Ads.   Targeted ads use sophisticated algorithms and "data mining" software (sometimes called "spyware") to analyze browser "cookies" - the little bits of data left on people's hard drives by websites they have visited. This analysis can usually provide a pretty good picture of what kinds of websites the surfer visits and give a good indication of his or her tastes, needs and/or desires. For example, if the data analyzed in a surfer's cookies indicated that they had visited a number of name brand stores online, the software used in targeted advertising might bring up a banner ad for a line of hats you're selling. Hopefully upon seeing the banner, the surfer will click your banner ad and come to your site.

While this type of marketing can be very effective, it's also very expensive. First, it usually requires an expert to set it up. Secondly, high-traffic digital property can be very expensive when it comes to renting ad space. The problem however is that targeted advertising of this type is really only effective when used on high-traffic sites.

E-mail marketing and solicitations have become a huge issue in recent years, and a number of laws regarding the practice of "spamming," (sending out unsolicited e-mail advertisements), are now on the books in several states. In fact, while being unethical, it really isn't effective and indeed may very well have the opposite effect of what is intended. In any event, reputable businesses no longer engage in this practice, if they ever did.

Since "spam" specifically refers to "unsolicited e-mail advertisements," it begs the question of just how an honest merchant is supposed to promote his or her wares and/or services without having to shell out for expensive targeted ads or search engine optimization. The good news is that there are affordable and low-cost options out there, although they have varying degrees of effectiveness.

There is a single legal loophole to all the "spam" rules: you may legally send a single (1) unsolicited e-mail to any address, which must contain a notice similar to this example: "This is a one-time communication. No further information will be sent to you at this e-mail address regarding this (product/service) unless you specifically request it by replying to info@LLC.COM." By doing this, you put the customer in control, and absolves you from any formal spam complaints. You should also be aware that even if a potential client chooses to receive mail from you, your messages must legally contain an "opt-out" link or a reply-to address the recipient can use to unsubscribe from any mailings.

Terms of Use or Service. You have probably become a member or used websites that actually have a Terms of Use or Terms of Service in place. A TOS, or Terms of Service, is quite different from a disclaimer. While a disclaimer disclaims, a TOS basically states the rules of using your site or service.

There are three main objectives you should have when creating your TOS. The first is that it must be understandable by the average person. A TOS that is full of legal jargon probably won't do you much good. Use everyday language. The second objective should be to make sure that your TOS is easily found on your site.

Many website owners include the TOS when a person registers for the website. After they have filled out the registration form, they are presented with the TOS, and it includes a checkbox that says that they have read and understand the TOS. If the site does not have any type of registration, the TOS may just be present, but may not require that a visitor gives any indication that they have read or understood the TOS.

In the second case, the words used in the TOS become more important. You must state that just by using your site that the visitor has automatically agreed to the TOS. Ideally, however, you will require your visitors to give some type of indication that they have read and do understand the TOS.

The third objective is to make sure that the TOS covers everything. Remember that this is a document designed to protect you from lawsuits down the road. The TOS should state what could go wrong, and what you will not be held liable for. It should also state how your visitors are expected to behave on your website. This is crucial for community websites, where customers interact with each other.

A Terms of Service agreement is typically used when the website offers some type of service, other than information. A Terms of Use agreement is typically used for information only type websites.

Here is a sample TOS/TOU:

"By using our website you are agreeing to comply with and be bound by the following terms of use. Review the terms carefully, and if you do not agree with them, do not use this website." The terms us, we, or our refers to Your Company, while the term you refers to the user or viewer of the site.

You agree to the terms and conditions as outlined in this Terms of Use Agreement with respect to our site. This agreement is the entire and only agreement between us and you, and it replaces any prior agreements you may have had with us, with respect to our site, products, services, and content. We reserve the right to change this agreement from time to time, without notification. The latest agreement will be posted on our website, and it is your responsibility to review the latest agreement.

This site is copyrighted by us. This copyright covers all content, organization, design, graphics, compilations, digital conversion, and magnetic translation that relates to this site. Copying this website, unless otherwise allowed, is a violation of our copyrights, and is strictly prohibited. You do not own any rights to any content on this website, unless it is your own work, such as messages you have written in our forum.

Ourcompany.com and others are our service marks or registered service marks or trademarks. Other product and company names mentioned on this site belong to their respective owners.

Privacy Policy

While a TOS may be very long and drawn out and very detailed, a Privacy Policy is typically more cut and dried. You absolutely must have a privacy policy, and many other sites that you do business with will actually require you to do so in order to use their service – such as a payment processing company for your website.

Here is a sample privacy policy:

"Thank you for visiting our website. This privacy policy is designed to inform you how information is collected from our site, and how that information is used.

Please read this privacy policy, in its entirety, before using our website, or submitting any personal information through our website.

By using our website, you are accepting the practices described in this privacy policy. These practices may be changed, and those changes will be posted on the website. All changes apply to practices moving forward, and do not affect the policies used in the past.

The privacy policy displayed here only pertains to this site. We link to other websites, and those websites have their own privacy policies. Our privacy policies do not pertain to their website, and their privacy policies do not pertain to our website.

We collect personally identifiable information, including names, postal addresses, and e-mail addresses. That information, however, is only obtained by us, when it is voluntarily submitted by you and our other visitors. If that information is provided to us, it is done so to help us fulfill your request. The information is only used to fulfill that request, unless you give us specific permission to use it in some other manner.

This site may use cookie and tracking technology, depending on the features offered. The use of cookies and tracking technology are needed for gathering information that includes the type of browser you are using, the type of operating system you are using, and in tracking the number of visitors to our site. This enables us to understand how visitors use our site, and how we can make changes that benefit our visitors.

Personal information cannot be collected with the use of cookies and tracking technology. The information gathered from the use of cookies and tracking technology on this website is used for internal information only, and not shared with others in any way that could personally identify our visitors.

We may share information with governmental agencies or other companies if they are assisting us in fraud prevention or investigation. We do this when it is permitted by law for us to do so, or when we are trying to protect against or prevent fraud or unauthorized transactions, or when we are investigating fraud that has already taken place. The information is not provided to any company for marketing purposes.

Your personally identifiable information that you provide is kept secure. Only authorized agents, contractors, and employees, who have also agreed to keep information shared with them confidential, can access this information. Any email or newsletters sent to you through our website are those that you requested, and each one will allow you the option of opting out of further mailings.

If you have problems, questions, concerns, or comments related to this privacy policy or our website, you may contact us at:

Our Company Street Address

City, Town, Zip Code Phone Number E-mail Address

We reserve the right to change this policy, if we find that changes are needed or warranted. All changes to this policy will be posted on our website." Again, you can adopt the privacy policy example to suit your own purposes.

Overall, when operating an online business, you must view everything from different angles. You must consider how information can be compromised, and also consider how your own content and services can be used against you from a legal standpoint. When you see problems that may occur, it is up to you to implement legal policy for your site that is designed to protect you – or to implement security measures designed to protect you and your customers or visitors.

Online business owners simply must see a bigger, wider picture than an average computer user sees. While you won't always catch every potential problem, if you follow the information in this guide, the chances are very good that you won't find yourself in the middle of a legal battle that pertains to your website or online business.

Your two main objectives should be to protect yourself, and to protect your customers!

Business Continuity Issues

In creating and building your business, there is no place for you to merely file an Article of Incorporation, create Operating Agreement, utilize partners and/or contractors or create a powerful and profitable brand only to set it and forget it. Instead, you must realize the legal zone of genius, comply with the local, state and federal regulators, appease your client and build wealth for yourself. At or about the same time, you must fully appreciate continual business continuity issues. While not meant to be exhaustive, the following are issues that you cannot ignore.

You should definitely consider how your business will handle returns. If you state that you are offering a product at a discount below the usual price, the discounted price must truly be lower than your regular price for the product. If you offer something for free, but in fact there are conditions to obtain the free item, you must disclose those conditions. According to the Federal Trade Commission (FTC), if you fail to follow these rules you are considered to be engaged in deceptive pricing practices.

You should provide sales receipts to your customers even if you are not legally required to do so for your particular online business. A receipt acts as a confirmation of your customer's order and helps document your customer's agreement to buy the listed goods at the listed price.

Technically, if a customer wants to return an item that is not defective, you are not legally obligated to take the item back. In practice, however, many online sellers, like traditional retailers, do allow returns. Often it's good for customer relations. In the online context, however, returns can be slightly more complicated, if for no other reason than that there are usually shipping costs to be considered. If you are willing to allow returns of non-defective merchandise, you should consider a policy requiring the buyer to pay return shipping. More generally, you should clearly state your return policy somewhere on your website.

Similarly, your company should note whether or not it offers warranties. Warranties are governed by the Uniform Commercial Code (UCC). Generally speaking, there are two types of warranties relating to the goods you sell: express warranties and implied warranties.

Express warranties are statements that you make, for example on your website, regarding the quality of the products you sell and your willingness to repair or otherwise remedy defects. A statement of this sort doesn't have to be labeled "Warranty" in order to be treated as a warranty under the law. You should exercise care in making any statements on your website that could be construed as express warranties and you will be held liable for the breach of those warranties.

Implied warranties exist regardless of whether you make any statements. Under basic commercial law, they arise whenever goods are sold. There are two types of implied warranties: the warranty of merchantability and the warranty of fitness for a particular purpose.

The warranty of merchantability is a warranty that a product is fit for ordinary purposes. For example, a wooden chair should be able to support the weight of a 250-pound person, a box of chocolates shouldn't contain metal shavings, and a microwave oven should have a timer. You should assume you will have some liability for a breach of this warranty, although you may be able to recover damages from the manufacturer.

The warranty of fitness for a particular purpose applies when you, as the seller, have reason to know that the goods being sold are to be used for a particular purpose, and the buyer is relying on your skill or judgment to select suitable goods. As an example, consider an online seller of paints who receives an e-mail from a potential buyer asking for a recommendation for paint to be used on a metal surface. If the seller recommends a paint that will only work on wood and actually damages metal surfaces, the seller will be liable for those damages.

Sales Tax. If you have a physical presence in a state, such as a store, office, or warehouse, you must collect sales tax from customers in that state. If you do not have a physical presence in the state, there is no requirement that you collect sales tax from customers in that state. In states where you are not required to collect sales tax, but where sales tax is due to the state, currently it is up to your customers to make sure the taxes are paid. Because online purchases have resulted in states receiving less revenue from sales tax, there has been an ongoing effort by states to require Internet-based businesses to do more to collect sales tax. Sales tax rules for online businesses may change in the future.

COMPLIANCE IS KEY

The most frequently asked question I get from my clients is, "How can I start my business and protect my assets?" The biggest challenge they face is operating their business and investing in their legal skills, knowledge, techniques, and toolkits so that they can protect their assets and also be in compliance with the laws, rules, and regulations that's required of them. And, I always challenge them to do good work.

My client's assets are a very common concern: their house, their cars, everything that they have built up so far. My main responsibility is to tell them about the legal rules and regulations of what they need to do so there is never a question as far as litigations go. Usually, you don't have to protect your assets by purchasing the most expensive strategies and solution. But you don't know that until you learn it through trials, tribulations or knowledge from a coach. I equip people with the knowledge of what the law expects so they can do the right thing at the right time for the right people.

Many people don't understand the proper rules and the regulations, what the pros and cons are, or what the law is really governing. I always hear my clients say, "Well, I'm told that I'm supposed to do x." I tell them that what you need to do is ask yourself what you want in your business, what solutions you want to offer, and what your message is. I can tell you what areas you need to very mindful of; for example, you can't sell people pipe dreams, because a lot of times, that's where the legal frustrations begin—when there are unmet expectations.

It is impossible to know everything about the law. Laws governing business change so much based on the facts and circumstances of our society. History has repeatedly shown that a federal agency's policing power of a certain issue will be powerful or emaciated based on the White House leanings or denials. Similarly, those in the U.S. Congress and Senate have allegiances, loyalties and their own agendas about what public policies should or should not be addressed during their term in office. In effect, the judicial branch gets its guidance on how to decide cases that become legal precedent for all other cases. Even at the State and local level, representatives in the legislative branch make promises to ward leaders, business men and those who wield the power of the purse that affects how we do business.

Accordingly, you cannot set up and then forget your business. Instead, you must stay abreast of what's being talked about at every level of government affecting your business. You should set Google Alerts, stay abreast of what's being talked about at your local Chamber of Commerce and even attend Town Hall Meetings. However, if you are not particular interested in the "legal mumbo jumbo," then you need to hire someone who is. Unfortunately, when it comes to law, ignorance isn't bliss nor is naiveté because as a business person you are expected to know the legalities governing your realities.

HELPFUL RESOURCES

As an attorney with more than twenty years of legal experience, I have a fiduciary obligation to advise you to seek legal advice about your specific issue. If, however, you do not have the funds to hire a lawyer or you want to do it yourself, there are both online and offline resource to assist you with creating, operating and protecting your business interests.

Federal Trade Commission: If you think your competitors are using unfair practices read through the FTC's online guide to Antitrust Laws. It provides information on how to report a suspected antitrust violation and whom to turn to for enforcement. There is sufficient information there to either avoid the necessity of hiring an attorney, or to be better prepared when you do hire one.

Small Business Administration: The SBA website has a page about handling legal concerns that links to some useful resources. It may be more useful to use the search box for articles and advice on specific issues. For example, a search for the term "sued by employee" turns up a number of useful articles on topics ranging from how to fire an employee without violating the law to buying business liability insurance.

Internal Revenue Service: If your legal issues are related to taxes you might find the information you need in the Small Business and Self-Employed Tax Center. The IRS maintains a collection of resources here, and some are available in Spanish as well.

U.S. Department of Justice: The Justice Dept. website has a list of free legal service providers. Choose a state and click through to find the ones near you. Most are oriented to helping individuals rather than small businesses, but it can't hurt to check.

Civil Rights Division of the Justice Dept.: For legal questions about the Americans with Disabilities Act visit the ADA Business Connection page. The Civil Rights Division of the Dept. of Justice has an extensive collection of information here about ADA compliance for customers and employees, and even has guidelines for some specific business types.

OSHA: If you have legal questions about your businesses compliance with OSHA regulations, what better place to get them answered than from OSHA itself? Use their, "Compliance Assistance Quick Start" program online.

For small businesses, they also offer a free, "On-Site Consultation Program," to help you determine if you're in compliance with the law.

SCORE: SCORE is a non-profit association that helps small businesses with advice, mentoring, and education. Its volunteers are experienced business people who provide free counseling by phone, email, and in person. The particular counselor or mentor you get will probably not be a lawyer, but it is possible that he or she will have had some experiences with the same legal issues you face, or can refer you to someone who has.

Use the "Find a Chapter" tool to locate the closest branch of the organization. They have more than 320 around the country. You can also search online for their legal guides.

Free Business Legal Clinics: There are various free legal clinics around the country. For example, the Small Business Legal Clinic in Oregon has had more than 300 attorneys volunteer for the SBLC Pro-Bono Project. To locate one near you, search online using terms like "free legal clinic" "business legal clinic" and the name of your state or locality.

Trade Associations: If you belong to a trade association you might get free legal advice for business, advice and help from their legal staff. If you don't yet belong to one, it might be worth the cost to join. Typically you'll at least get online and newsletter-based legal advice. Check a list of trade organizations to find the one that makes the most sense for your small business.

Your Network: While you shouldn't rely too heavily on the legal opinions of non-lawyers, it is possible that other business owners have had the same legal issues you're facing. Ask around, and to see how they resolved matters. You'll be better prepared if and when you hire an attorney to help you. Better preparation cuts down on those billable hours you'll be paying for.

BUSINESS LAW DOCUMENTS

The following is a list of documents you need to run, monetize and protect your business:

Independent Contractor Agreement

Nondisclosure Agreements

Terms of Use & Privacy Agreements

Software Licensing & Development Agreements

Operating Agreement

Partnership Agreement

Licensing Agreement

Non-Competition Agreement

Consultant Agreement

Copyright Transfer Agreement

Sales/Service Agreement

Employment Agreement

Succession Planning Documents

Small Business Retirement Plans

Asset Protection Agreements

- Privacy Policy
- Terms and Conditions
- Copyright Policy
- Return and Refund Policy

BUSINESS PROTECTION STRATEGIES

The following is simple step-by-step guide to help you create run, monetize and protect your business:

1. Create a business that solves a problem.

2. Share your brilliance to help people view you as an expert.

3. Choose a business structure that suits you.

4. Keep your business and personal assets separate.

5. Find right partners, team and/or board members.

6. Keep good business records and observe necessary formalities.

7. Document all major business decisions and put them in your corporate book.

8. Sign and keep copies of the contracts your company enters (internally among owners and employees and externally with vendors and suppliers).

9. Review and update your operating agreement (LLCs) or bylaws (corporations).

10. Create and maintain a membership (LLCs) or stock (corporations) transfer ledger so you always know who owns what portion of the company.

11. Protect your business assets and intellectual property.

12. Respect the rules, regulations and regulators.

NEXT STEPS

Someone once said that we coach based on what we experienced which rings true to me since my ideal client tends to be someone who is committed to be a change maker in their homes, families and in their communities. I love to educate, edify and empower people who have big dreams and big goals and are committed to make a big difference in their lives. Similarly, my ideal client realizes and appreciates that they have what it takes to make their business dreams a reality. I'm available to assist you if you

- Want to build and live your dream life.
- Want to create a purpose-driven business
- Want to monetize your brilliance like a boss.

Let's connect!

Gift: mstonimooregift.com

Social Media: @mstonimoore #legallychic #savvyceo

ABOUT THE AUTHOR

Toni Moore, Esquire, is a Lawyer and Business Development Strategist who is personally committed to helping women own their power to design their business, life, story, and destiny. Through the years, Toni has cultivated her inspirational message of hope to encourage women to use their brilliance to create the business and life they desire.

Toni graduated from the University of Pennsylvania and Temple University Beasley School of Law wherein she received her Juris Doctorate and Master's in Taxation (LLM). Toni Moore is a licensed attorney in the States of Pennsylvania and New Jersey, teaches nonprofit compliance and public policy. Toni once maintained a PA/NJ insurance license, mortgage broker's license, and Series 6, 63, and 26 Investment Licenses. Toni shares her brilliance as an author, speaker and coach and is available for booking.